Is MONETARISM
Enough?

IS MONETARISM ENOUGH?

Essays in refining and reinforcing
the monetary cure for inflation

PATRICK MINFORD   ●   HAROLD ROSE

WALTER ELTIS   ●   MORRIS PERLMAN

JOHN BURTON

With contributions by

Michael Beenstock · Samuel Brittan
Alan Budd · Tim Congdon
Anthony Courakis · William Keegan
Russell Lewis · Hamish McRae
William Rees-Mogg · John B. Wood

Chairman: **Arthur Seldon**

Published by
The Institute of Economic Affairs
1980

(I EA readings ; 24)

First published in September 1980 by
THE INSTITUTE OF ECONOMIC AFFAIRS
ISSN 0305-814X
ISBN 0-255 36131-9

Printed in England by
Goron Pro-Print Co. Ltd., Lancing, West Sussex
Set in Monotype Times Roman 11 on 12 point

Contents

Preface

The IEA *Readings* have been devised to refine the market in economic thinking by presenting varying approaches to a single theme. They are intended primarily for teachers and students of economics but are edited to help non-economists who want to know how economics can explain their activities.

Readings 24 is based on an experiment in conducting a small-scale Seminar with an audience of 14 economists and editors and treating the proceedings as an interchange of expertise between the formal speakers and the informal responses.

The subject was the conditions under which monetary control of the economy to master inflation could work most effectively. Professors Patrick Minford and Harold Rose and Mr Walter Eltis analysed the macro-economic conditions; and Mr Morris Perlman discussed micro-economic controls on government expenditure by pricing as affecting the conduct of macro-controls; Mr John Burton considered the power of the trade unions to 'cause' inflation.

The audience comprised:

Samuel Brittan—Economics Editor, *Financial Times*

Alan Budd—Research Fellow in Banking, London Graduate School of Business Studies

Michael Beenstock—Senior Research Fellow, London Graduate School of Business Studies

A. S. Courakis—Brasenose College, Oxford

George Cardona—HM Treasury

Tim Congdon—Messell & Co.

Colin Jones—Editor, *Banker*

William Keegan—*Observer*

Nigel Lawson—Financial Secretary, Treasury

Rodney Lord—City Office, *Daily Telegraph*

Russell Lewis—Features Writer, *Daily Mail*

Hamish McRae—Financial Editor, *Guardian*

William Rees-Mogg—Editor, *The Times*

Is Monetarism Enough?

Robert Thomas—Partner, W. Greenwell & Co.

John B. Wood—Institute of Economic Affairs

The Minford, Rose and Eltis papers led to closely-argued discussion on technical aspects of the control of the money supply. The Perlman paper on micro-controls on the whole doubted the relevance for macro-controls of a pricing discipline on the demand for government services (although conceding the case for charging on efficiency grounds), a view disputed by Professor Minford, Dr Budd, Dr Courakis and from the Chair.

The exchanges have produced authoritative and stimulating reflections on a subject of central importance to government policy in removing inflation from the economic system.

July 1980   ARTHUR SELDON

1. Monetarism, Inflation and Economic Policy

PATRICK MINFORD

University of Liverpool

The Author

A. P. L. MINFORD: Edward Gonner Professor of Applied Economics, University of Liverpool, since 1976. Formerly Visiting Hallsworth Research Fellow, University of Manchester, 1974-75. Sometime Consultant to the Ministry of Overseas Development, Ministry of Finance (Malawi), Courtaulds, Treasury, British Embassy (Washington). Editor of *National Institute Economic Review,* 1975-76. Author of *Substitution Effects, Speculation and Exchange Rate Stability* (1978), and of essays published in *Inflation in Open Economies* (1976); *The Effects of Exchange Adjustments* (1977); *On How to Cope with Britain's Trade Position* (1977); *Contemporary Economic Analysis* (1978). Contributed a paper, 'Macro-economic Controls on Government', to the IEA's Seminar *The Taming of Government* (IEA Readings No. 21, 1979).

I. INTRODUCTION

In the last decade, inflation has become embedded in the British economy at rates of 10 per cent or more, whereas in the 1960s it rarely exceeded 5 per cent and in the 1950s ranged between 1 and 3 per cent. Chart 1 shows the UK and the industrial world's inflation rates since the early 1950s. Our experience has been matched on the average by other industrial countries, though their acceleration in prices after 1972 was less than that in the UK.

Parallel with this price acceleration, there has been a rise in budget deficits as a percentage of national income and also in the rate of growth of the money supply (Charts 2 and 3).

I shall be arguing that the strong associations between these three magnitudes is not coincidental, but that there is a powerful body of economic theory predicting them. That theory can be shown to be consistent with rational or maximising behaviour by economic agents, and to have to its credit empirical success in predicting actual behaviour both in individual markets and in aggregates of markets.[1]

Of necessity I shall select aspects most closely relevant to the topic of inflation.

II. FIXED EXCHANGE RATES:[2] A COMPLICATION

Let me first dispose of a complication. Up to 1971, this country and many others were on fixed exchange rates. This system had the weight of the Bretton Woods international financial agreement between all major countries behind it and prevented governments from changing the price of their currency except in specific and unusual circumstances. The result was that, except in these circum-

---

[1] Minford [1980] discusses the theory at length and gives many of the major references. Also Lucas and Sargent [1979] for a recent account of the state of macro-economic theory.

[2] Many of the major papers setting out this 'monetary approach to the balance of payments' are assembled in Frenkel and Johnson [1976].

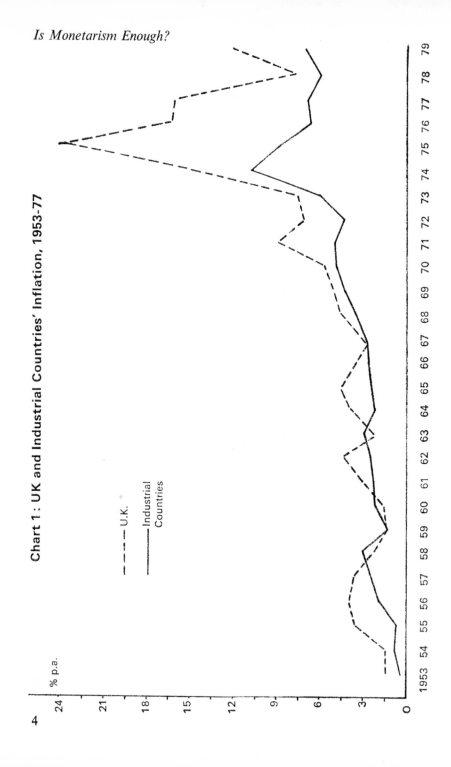

Chart 1: UK and Industrial Countries' Inflation, 1953-77

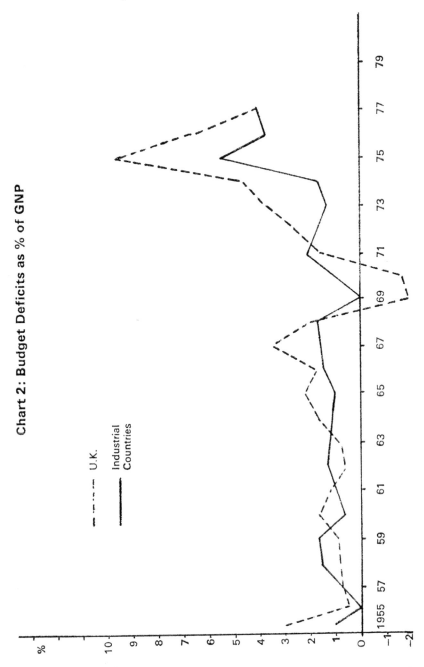

Chart 2: Budget Deficits as % of GNP

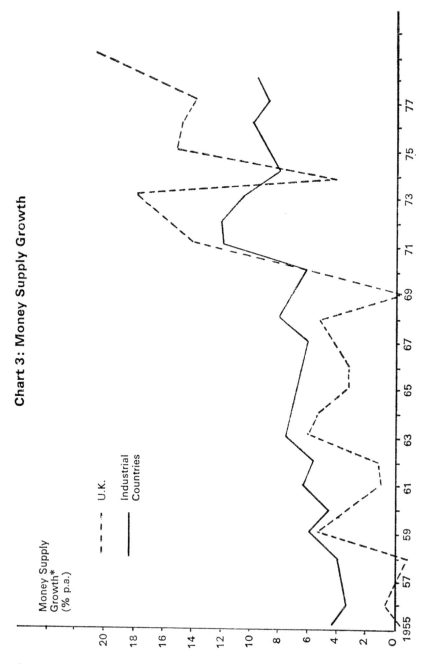

Chart 3: Money Supply Growth

stances, governments had to pursue policies which would keep their national price level in line with the price levels of others; otherwise their goods would cease to be, or become excessively, competitive in international markets, causing corrective mechanisms to be set in train. Hence, broadly speaking, up to 1971 each country's inflation rate was dictated by the prevailing international inflation rate. The UK was no exception, as Chart 1 reveals; until 1968 our inflation was close to the world rate; then, owing to the large 1967 devaluation, our inflation began to drift upwards and away from the world rate.

USA exported inflation via deficits, 1950-71

We have, therefore, to look for the causes of world inflation during that period in the policies of the dominant economy of that time, the USA. Briefly, that period is chronicled in Table I which shows the rise in the US budget deficits between 1950 and 1971, and the consequent rise in its balance-of-payments deficit; this led to a loss of foreign exchange reserves which, flowing into the central banks of Western Europe, increased their rates of monetary expansion, and so the rate of world monetary expansion. World inflation in response to these developments rose to 6 per cent by 1971.

TABLE I

MONEY SUPPLY, DEFICITS AND INFLATION UNDER FIXED EXCHANGE RATES, 1953-59 TO 1971

Average	*1953-59*	*1960-65*	*1966-71*	*1971*
US Budget Deficit (% of GDP)	0·6	0·7	1·1	2·3
Other 'Big 9' Budget Deficit (% of GDP)	1·6	0·9	1·15	1·3
US Balance of Payments Deficit ($bn. p.a.)	1·4	2·0	6·4	29·7
Other 'Big 9' Central Banks' rise in $ reserves ($bn. p.a.)	0·9	1·0	5·8	27·4
World Money Supply Growth (% p.a.)	5·5	7·8	8·6	11·8
World Inflation (% p.a.)	2·8	3·8	5·1	5·9

I have no space here to discuss the detailed mechanisms involved because I wish to turn to the present international framework, that of floating exchange rates.

III. FLOATING EXCHANGE RATES: THE PRESENT CASE

Whereas fixed exchange rates imposed limitations on government policies, no such limitations are imposed under floating, since the exchange rate can depreciate if domestic prices rise more rapidly than overseas prices or appreciate if they rise less rapidly.[3] How would policies affect the economy under this exchange-rate régime?

Consider a rise in the budget deficit because of a rise in public spending. The direct effect is to raise the demand for goods and services. This of course is the effect stressed by Keynes and his disciples in their advocacy of 'public works' as a means of combating depression.[4]

Supply-side effects

There are, however, other effects. In the present-day economy—whatever may have been the case in the 1930s, a debate I cannot enter here[5]—it cannot be assumed that the short-run supply of these goods and services will be available at a constant relative price. Theory indeed suggests that suppliers will require rising relative prices to increase supply, except in the case of imported goods presumed available at the international price. In the labour market, the evidence for the UK—perhaps because of high unionisation, widespread minimum wage provisions, and generous social security benefits relative to earnings—suggests rather weak responses of relative wages to

---

[3] For a review of the theory of floating exchange rates, see Mussa [1979].

[4] Keynes [1936]; Howson and Winch [1977] provide a fascinating account of Keynes's pre-war activities as a policy adviser. The *NIESR Reviews* since the early 1960s exemplify the post-war policy advice derived from the standard interpretation of Keynes. The 're-interpretations' of Leijonhufvud [1968] and others since nevertheless preserve the *rationale* for the anti-depression policy prescription.

[5] Keynes postulated an upward-sloping supply curve for output, but regarded nominal wages as highly insensitive to labour market conditions; hence his analysis was entirely in 'wage units'.

demand pressures. However, limited observations of the secondary labour market or 'cash economy' in the UK, as in Italy where it is even larger, suggest that these demand pressures cause sharp changes in real wages in this sector.

In the goods market, the evidence has been contested in quarterly data, on the one hand by Godley, Nordhaus and Coutts [1978] who maintain that demand has no effect on 'normal' profit margins in the UK and, on the other, by a wide variety of UK and international studies which appear to show demand effects on prices (Laidler and Parkin [1975]). The UK debate has been clouded by an unfortunate confusion between the demand variable and the normalisation process carried out by Godley *et al.* This confusion appears to be avoided in annual data where we have obtained the following equation over the full post-war period, which indicates very clear and strong demand effects on relative prices (Table II).

TABLE II

PRICE EQUATION

log (PRICE LEVEL)=4·6 + ·24 log (WAGE LEVEL)
        (·49) (·11)

+ ·76 log (WORLD PRICE LEVEL×£ EXCHANGE RATE)
  (·11)

+ 1·9 log (RATIO OF GNP TO TREND)
  (·59)

+ ·015 TIME TREND
  (·002)

3 STAGE LEAST SQUARES. Standard errors bracketed.

DW=1·28. Q=9·7. SEE=·052. R^2=·79. Annual data 1956-76

In the long run, I should add, supply must be totally inelastic, a proposition hardly disputed.[6]

In the first place, therefore, we have to consider these supply-side effects of the increased budget deficit.

---

[6] In other words, the economy has some level of 'potential' (or equilibrium) output which is independent of the level of domestic demand; with it go equilibrium levels of real wages, the terms of trade, profit margins and real

[*Continued on page 10*]

IV. FINANCING THE DEFICIT

Secondly, the deficit increase must be *financed,* both in the short and in the long run.

The government deficit creates financial assets (claims on the government) which someone, at home or abroad, must be prepared to hold in their portfolios. If no-one is willing to hold these assets, they must be spent. They will continue to be spent until they *are* held.

According to Keynes, the extra demand created by the budget deficit would bring forth extra supply, which in turn would create savings. These savings would then finance the deficits. Thus, for him and his disciples, the counterpart of the expansion in output provides the solution of the financial problem.

Suppose, however, that output cannot be significantly increased because of supply inelasticity. Suppose too that there is a strict limit on the possibilities of foreigners taking up these claims on government. Then too there is an inelasticity of the savings that could finance the deficit. In other words, the extra financial assets will not be demanded.

Inflation as equilibrating force

How is this impasse solved? We have observed that these assets would be spent. The effects of this extra demand, in the absence of additional supplies, must be continuously rising prices until the assets are held. In short, the only condition under which a continuous flow of additional government financial assets will be absorbed by private agents will be one of higher inflation. The rise in inflation causes existing stocks of financial assets fixed in money terms to

[*Continued from page 9*]

interest rates. We may call this the sustainable level of supply. Provided the economy tends towards this state if disturbed, we may also refer to it as the long-run state. The vast majority of economists would accept the proposition in the text; there are, however, those who would dispute that the economy tends towards such a state (i.e. is 'stable') if not pushed there by government intervention, notably the Cambridge Economic Policy Group: *CEPG Reviews* (1975 onwards). Some economists (e.g. Blinder and Solow [1973]) have questioned this stability property for budget deficits financed *without* monetary expansion, but do not question it in general. To deal with the CEPG 'minority view', which rests on a high degree of 'market failure', would take us too far afield here.

drop in real value; consequently holders need to acquire the additional assets injected by the government in order to restore their holdings of assets to their equilibrium values. It turns out therefore that under these assumptions a higher budget deficit results in higher inflation.[7]

But, it may be said with some justice, these are long-run assumptions; in the short run output has some elasticity in supply, and foreigners may lend to the government as the counterpart of a temporary balance-of-payments deficit. If it takes a long time to reach the 'long run', then surely it will be a long time before the inflation occurs; by then the situation may be different, and meanwhile we will enjoy the beneficial effects on output of the higher deficit.

It requires only common sense to see that such a Micawber-like attitude is fraught with dangers. Presumably we are not indifferent to the long run, and presumably we cannot *systematically* count on something turning up to bail us out of the long-run consequences of our actions.

Expectations

But there are more immediate problems, too. Markets and decisions are linked inter-temporally. The expectation of what will happen tomorrow influences today's behaviour and events. In particular the long-run inflationary consequence will be anticipated when the budget deficit is raised.[8] This in turn will raise long-term interest rates, as lenders require compensation for the loss of purchasing power of their capital loaned out; and, as interest rates rise, existing holders of debt will experience a capital loss, which will tend to make them spend *less* in order to rebuild their asset positions.

---

[7] This process, if 'money' is substituted for 'financial assets', is the 'real balance effect', first described by Patinkin [1965]. However, the process applies here to all financial assets issued by government, and is best termed the 'portfolio balance effect': Minford [1980], Matthews and Minford [1980].

[8] This assumes that expectations are 'rational', i.e. that agents work out from available information how the economy is likely to behave. This does *not* imply that *each* agent works it out separately; clearly specialisation occurs in information gathering and analysis, and agents buy forecasts, etc. Nor does it imply that there is 'full' information available; the point is that, given whatever information *is* publicly available, forecasts are 'optimal'. A topical account is in Lucas and Sargent [1979].

But private agents will not merely infer the long-run consequences of the higher deficit. They will also be in a position to work out the short-run consequences—the path by which the economy will adjust itself to the policy change. There will be a number of conflicting influences on this path. On the one hand, the higher public sector demand for goods will put upward pressure on output; on the other, the worsened financial asset position of private agents will lower their demands for goods. Finally, the supply side inelasticity will dampen to a greater or lesser extent the net impact of these demand effects on *actual* output while the balance-of-payments effect will also depend on the interaction of these pressures. To generalise from a large number of simulations over different starting values we have carried out for a model of the UK of this sort, the output and balance-of-payments paths seem *not* to correspond to the Keynesian analysis; output either is negligibly affected or may even drop in the short run in response to the higher deficit.[9]

But, if so, the financing problem will also be acute in the short run. The counterpart savings will not be available. Consequently, the only way in which the additional assets created by the government can be absorbed is through higher inflation in the short run also.

In brief, a higher government deficit causes higher inflation and reduces (or, as it is sometimes put, 'crowds out') private spending in the short as well as in the long run.

In work over the past five years, several of us at Liverpool University have been trying to establish empirically the relationships implicit in the above analysis. We have had a limited success in so far as we can say that the 'predictive record' of the resulting model when used to 'forecast' the past is certainly no worse and on inflation rather better than that of respectable economic forecasters[10] (Table III).

---

[9] Many details are given in Minford [1980].

[10] These forecasters were forecasting the future, whereas our model has been estimated with the benefit of hindsight (even though its 'forecasts' are made on the basis of the same data as available to the forecasters). This gives the model an advantage. But it is also at a disadvantage: forecasters supplement their models with other information (they 'adjust the residuals' of their equations); but our model has to forecast unaided by such adjustments. Both the model and the forecasters make their forecasts on unchanged 'policies', i.e. their best guess about what policies for the future *are*. On balance the comparison, though crude, is perhaps not unfair.

TABLE III

MODEL (& NIESR)
ERROR IN FORECASTING ONE YEAR AHEAD, 1959-76

Inflation (% p.a.)		*Model error*	*NIESR error*
Whole period	1959-76	2·4	n.a.
Fixed period	1959-70	1·9	3·1 (1966-70, other n.a.)
Floating period 1971-76		3·5	6·5
Output (% of actual)			
Whole period	1959-76	2·5	n.a.
Fixed period	1959-70	2·7	1·3 (1964-70)
Floating period 1971-76		1·8	3·6

If we can say that the model picks up some broad influences on inflation and output in the UK, what does it predict for the effects of a rise in the budget deficit?

The model suggests that a rise in the budget deficit causes a rise in inflation within a year of its occurring, and does *not* raise output in the manner predicted by Keynes and his disciples (Chart 4).

V. ROLE OF MONETARY POLICY

I now want to step back and consider a complication in the analysis —monetary policy. The financial assets issued as the counterpart of the deficit are of two kinds, money and government debt carrying a rate of interest. In the previous analysis, I have implicitly assumed that both types of asset grow at the same rate, and that there is no attempt to induce the private sector to hold more government debt and so to hold the growth rate of the money supply down below the rate warranted by the deficit. Some economists have, however, argued that control of the money supply can be achieved *without* control of the deficit and that this would be sufficient to control inflation.[11]

---

[11] Such has been the theme of the main line of Chicago monetarists, such as Friedman [1968]; Andersen and Carlsen [1968]. They have, however, usually added that governments have not been prepared in practice to tolerate sufficiently high real interest rates to achieve such monetary independence for long.

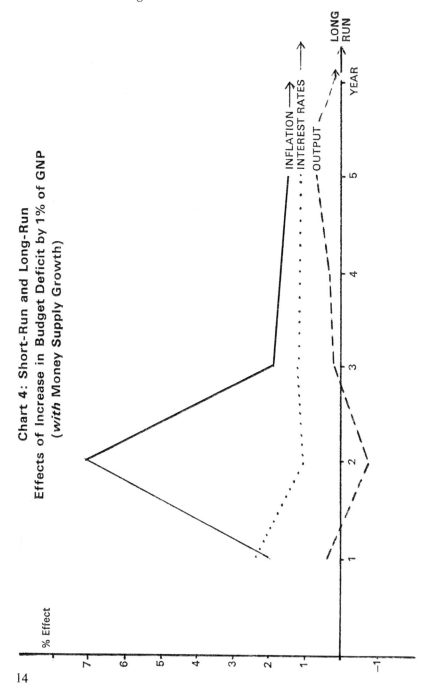

Chart 4: Short-Run and Long-Run
Effects of Increase in Budget Deficit by 1% of GNP
(*with* Money Supply Growth)

Chart 5: Short-run Effects of Increase in Budget Deficit by 1% of GNP (*without* Money Supply Growth until Year 4)

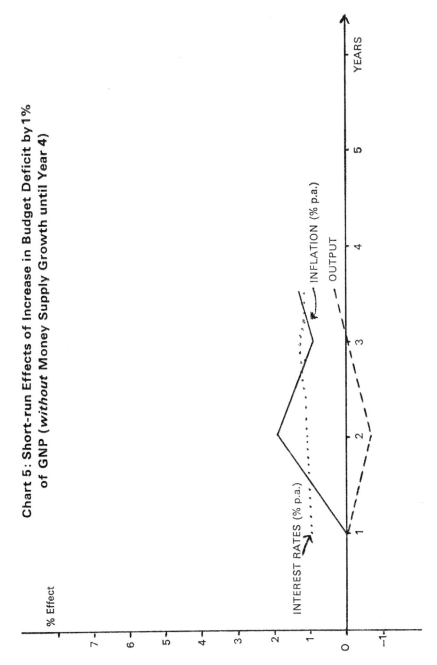

I have to agree with them that this is a theoretical possibility *for a short period.* I show below a simulation of the effects of the same rise in the budget deficit *unaccompanied* by any rise in the money supply for an illustrative three-year period (Chart 5).

It can be seen that the ceiling on monetary growth does prevent inflation rising so much in the first three years of the policy. Since inflation is expected to rise, however, interest rates rise causing private spending to drop. The result is that output still does not rise in the short run in a Keynesian manner; instead private agents save more and finance the government deficit because they need to rebuild their financial assets.

Monetary policy muffler

Hence, the monetary policy only *muffles initially,* so to speak, the underlying effects of the rise in the deficit. Furthermore, there are in any case grave doubts as to whether it is possible to hold down monetary growth effectively in this way even for as long as three years, when all other financial assets are expanding more rapidly. Our econometric estimates of demand for money relationships were not made in circumstances like these; and recent experience suggests that if *systematic* attempts are made to exploit these estimated relationships in a way that penalises holders of money, unsuspected institutional change designed to help substitution out of money will occur. Monetary growth is then held down, but its intended effect is evaded.[12]

A possible response is that the definition of money should be widened to include such items as building society deposits or that several definitions of money should be made monetary target variables (as has occurred in the USA over various periods). I am sympathetic to the spirit of these suggestions but the widening leads inexorably to the widest definition of all, the government deficit as the source of the financial asset injection.

---

[12] The basis of this argument is in Lucas [1970], that behaviour and expectations are conditional on the policy régimes and other exogenous processes in existence. Dr Charles Goodhart has popularised it, in the context of UK monetary relationships, as 'Goodhart's Law'.

VI. ROLE OF STABILISATION POLICY

This leads me to my last related topic: How far can the budget deficit be used as a short-term instrument for *stabilising* national output? We are to imagine that the budget is balanced for a 'normal' year, that is, a year when output is at its normal level. When output falls below its normal level, however, the budget deficit rises for two reasons: first, because when incomes fall revenues fall and social security benefits rise; second, because the government deliberately lowers tax rates or spends more to stimulate output.[13] Since the budget is balanced in an average year, there is no *average* effect on inflation from this policy; and in so far as the policy is successful in holding up output in recessions, it provides the counterpart savings necessary to finance the deficits in these recessions, so there should be little significant inflation effect even when there is a deficit. If we strengthen the policy by holding money supply growth constant, then it would appear it can give the best of both worlds—inflation and output stability, or at least more of it than otherwise.

Again, there is little doubt in my mind that this is an important *theoretical possibility*. I illustrate it (Chart 6) with a further simulation which shows the path of output relative to 'normal' predicted by the model from 1977 onwards under the twin assumptions of a stabiliser policy and of no such policy.

Chart 6 shows that there is some modest improvement in output stability. It also turns out that there is no significant cost in inflation instability.

The questions, however, as before, revolve around the *practical* problems in this course.

Identifying equilibrium—what and where is a 'normal year'?

The major difficulty is that of identifying a normal year or normal output.[14] An analogous problem arises in commodity price stabilisa-

---

[13] There is an informal discussion of the theoretical issues surrounding this effect in Minford [1979]. Great care has to be taken to distinguish deliberately planned fiscal deficits and unexpected deviations from plans. The former ('activist' or feedback stabilisation) are particularly vulnerable to the practical objections raised below. The latter ('automatic' or 'passive' stabilisation) should be random events, and so are not dangerous in the same way.

[14] This is not quite the same as, though it has a clear family resemblance to, Friedman's 'long and variable lags' [1968]. The problem identified here is not that of how the economy responds, but of where the economy is relative to equilibrium. Brunner and Meltzer [1979] have voiced a similar worry.

Chart 6: Hypothetical Behaviour of Output from 1978, with and without Stabilisers

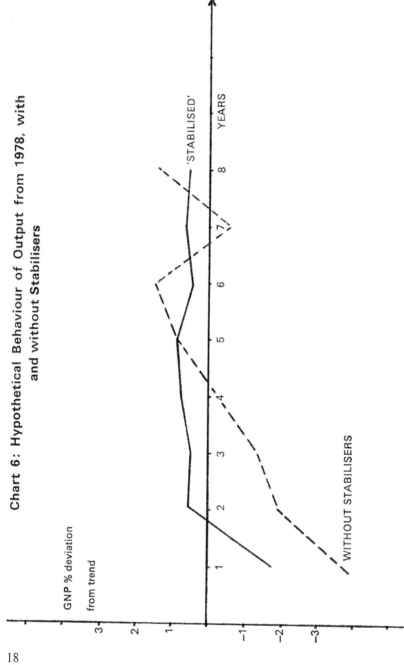

tion schemes where the managers of the intervention fund have to decide what the equilibrium price is. We know there is such a thing but we have inadequate information, as mere observers of the broad scene, to determine it. It is an unobservable quantity and over time we are likely to discover new information that leads us continuously to revise our previous view of what it *was*. Hence it is quite possible for governments to aim, for example, to hold unemployment down for a long period to a level that they later recognise was too low, i.e. lower than the minimum necessary for normal labour-market functioning; indeed in the UK and the USA there have been substantial upward revisions of this sort, but only *after* governments have pursued policies which were strongly expansionary at times of excess demand.

I illustrate this problem by comparing the results of the same stabiliser rule on different assumptions about the government's (and other forecasters') errors in their estimate of normal output (Table IV).

TABLE IV

STANDARD ERROR OF GNP AROUND ITS TREND, WITH STABILISATION MISTAKES ABOUT TREND LEVEL

% Error About Trend	*No Stabilisation Policy*	*Active Stabilisation*
0	2·8*	0·7*
1	2·8	0·8
2	2·8	1·8
3	2·8	2·8
4	2·8	3·7
5	2·8	4·6

* Case illustrated in Chart 6.

As one would obviously expect, the mistake in identifying the equilibrium level of output worsens the result of stabilisation policy. It turns out that a mistake of only 3 per cent is sufficient in this 'active' case to wipe out the gains of stabilisation. Larger mistakes cause clear worsening on the no-stabilisation outcome.

Rise in deficit self-sustaining

There is another problem. Experience and econometric analysis show that a rise in the deficit is self-sustaining. What goes up only comes down by accident, so to speak; formally, the UK deficit can be reasonably described by a 'random walk' (perhaps with upward drift).[15] The reason in political economy is presumably the inertia imparted by vested interests: you raise spending this year; group A, who benefited then, regard it as a right next year and subsequently, to be defended by their votes and lobbying. Therefore, a government may with the best will raise the deficit in a bad year, but will find it politically difficult to lower in a good year, let alone in a normal year. The consequence is that 'stabiliser' policies give an inbuilt upward bias to the government deficit and so to inflation.

I therefore conclude that the impressive theoretical case for stabilisers had better be treated with the greatest practical reserve. The limit to which one might go in allowing it scope would be to set a small band of permitted variation around the budget deficit (perhaps $\frac{1}{4}$ per cent or so of national income) to allow for unanticipated shortfalls or over-spending as compared with the declining target values set by a government's financial plan.

VII. SHIFTING SERVICES INTO THE MARKET SECTOR

This is uncomfortable advice, particularly for people such as us academics in the public sector. The stark truth is that, if we wish to restore a sound currency in our society, very substantial cuts—to the tune of at least 4 per cent of national income—must be made in the present government's borrowing, the Public Sector Borrowing Requirement (PSBR). How? One way, which it seems right to reject because of its effect on incentives,[16] would be to raise taxes by this amount. That leaves public spending. No doubt there is some 'waste' to be rooted out by the vigilant saving of candle-ends, the

---

[15] Based on annual data, 1956-77.

[16] More precisely, the effect is to increase *distortions* because of the substitution effects between leisure and goods. Whether people 'work harder' is not at issue, since this depends upon the income-elasticity of demand for leisure, which has no bearing on the welfare effects of taxation.

reduction of over-manning, the introduction eventually of computerisation, and so forth. But it is easy to be over-optimistic on this score.

The choice then is effectively to cut the scale of services or to charge for a larger proportion of them. My colleagues in the profession have contributed a large and growing literature on the effects of using prices to allocate resources;[17] the evidence overwhelmingly shows that goods and services, if provided free, are wasted, but if charged at economic prices are allocated to those with the greatest need for them. For those in most need, who possess inadequate income, the correct remedy is an income subsidy, or the 'negative income tax', but it is wrong to waste resources by giving them away not only to such people but also to those who can well afford them and would happily pay for them.

It is a sad irony of the present situation that much wanted public services are being cut back, when a willingness to allow the public to *pay* for their retention would allow them to survive healthily.

VIII. CONCLUSIONS

Let me re-state the main propositions I have tried to establish:

1. Inflation is caused by budget deficits.

2. Stabilisation policy is potentially dangerous and should be limited to placing an error band around the budget target.

3. Monetary policy cannot be systematically independent of the budget deficit.

4. Budget deficits should be cut by increasing the proportion of public services for which economic charges are levied, whilst maintaining income subsidies to the least well-off.

---

[17] Appeal is made here to micro-economic theory and applied work in its broadest sense—to be found in any good micro-economic textbook. See Seldon [1977] and references he cites on the issues specific to UK public expenditure.

REFERENCES

Andersen, L. C., and Carlsen, K. M. [1970], 'A monetarist model for economic stabilisation', FRB-St. Louis, April.

Blinder, A. S., and Solow, R. M. [1973], 'Analytical Foundation of Fiscal Policy', in Blinder, Solow *et al.*, *The Econometrics of Public Finance,* Brookings Institution, Washington D.C.

Brunner, K., and Meltzer, A. H. [1979], 'Guiding Principles for Monetary Policy', Paper presented to 1979 Konstanz Seminar on Monetary Theory and Policy, University of Rochester (mimeo).

Cambridge Economic Policy Group [1975-79], *Economic Policy Reviews,* Department of Applied Economics, Cambridge.

Frenkel, J. A., and Johnson, H. G. (eds.) [1976], *The Monetary Approach to the Balance of Payments*, Allen and Unwin.

Friedman, M. [1968], 'The Role of Monetary Policy', *American Economic Review,* 58, pp. 1-17.

Godley, W. A., Nordhaus, W. D., and Coutts, K. [1978], *Industrial Pricing in the UK,* Cambridge University Press.

Howson, S., and Winch, D. [1977], *The Economic Advisory Council: 1930-1939,* Cambridge University Press.

Keynes, J. M. [1936], *The General Theory of Employment, Interest and Money,* Macmillan.

Laidler, D. W., and Parkin, M. J. [1975], 'Inflation: A Survey', *Economic Journal,* December.

Leijonhufvud, A. [1968], *Of Keynesian Economics and the Economics of Keynes,* Oxford University Press, New York.

Lucas, R. E. [1970], 'Econometric testing of the natural rate hypothesis', in O. Eckstein (ed.), *The Econometrics of Price Determination,* Federal Reserve Board of Governors, Washington D.C.

Lucas, R. E., and Sargent, T. J. [1979], 'After Keynesian Macroeconomics', in *After the Phillips Curve: Persistence of High Inflation and High Unemployment,* Conference Series No. 19, Federal Reserve Bank of Boston.

Matthews, K. G. P., and Minford, A. P. L. [1980], 'Asset acquisition —an integrated portfolio approach to private sector expenditure and financial asset accumulation', *Journal of Money, Credit and Banking* (forthcoming).

Minford, A. P. L. [1979], 'Macroeconomic controls on Government', in A. Seldon (ed.), *The Taming of Government*, IEA Readings No. 21, Institute of Economic Affairs, London.

——, [1980], 'A rational expectations model of the UK under fixed and floating exchange rates', in K. Brunner and A. H. Meltzer (eds.), *The State of Macroeconomics*, Carnegie-Rochester Conference on Public Policy Series, No. 12, Supplement to *Journal of Monetary Economics,* North-Holland.

Mussa, M. [1979], 'Empirical Regularities in the Behaviour of Exchange Rates & Theories of the Foreign Exchange Market', in K. Brunner and A. H. Meltzer (eds.), *Policies for Employment, Prices and Exchange Rates*, Carnegie-Rochester Conference Series on Public Policy No. 11, Supplement to *Journal of Monetary Economics.*

Patinkin, D. [1965], *Money, Interest and Prices* (2nd Edition), Harper and Row, New York.

Seldon, A. [1977], *Charge,* Temple Smith, London.

Questions and Discussion

SAMUEL BRITTAN: An implication of Patrick Minford's paper is that the issue of financial assets by government, even if they are not called money, is inflationary and that after about three years—even if the government finances them entirely by bonds—there would be an inflationary effect. What is so special about government? Why does inflation not result from an issue of a vast amount of private bonds?

MINFORD: The quick answer is that the private sector issue of bonds is matched by a private sector acquisition of assets, so they cancel out. Any financial assets issued by the private sector cancel out with other private liabilities acquired by the private sector and thus do not affect aggregate private sector spending behaviour.

BRITTAN: Suppose ICI has a bond issue this year. It is then nationalised—but nothing else changes. It has another bond issue next year which is called government security. Does that bond issue then become more inflationary?

MINFORD: That is a different question. It depends on the *reason* for nationalisation. For example, if ICI was making losses and the bond issue was made to finance them, it would be on the same basis as other government deficit financing. In general, the relationship between deficits, monetary growth, and inflation will depend upon institutional arrangements, such as the extent to which public enterprises are truly commercial and the division of saving between the public and private sectors. If these change, the relationships may change.

MICHAEL BEENSTOCK: Patrick Minford did not emphasise a very important point in his paper: bonds do have an independent inflationary effect. In the early days, when we all became born-again monetarists, it was nice to latch on to something like the money supply or M3 as somehow a very simplified way of thinking about the process, to give the politicians and other people something to think about. But we have now moved into a more sophisticated age of thinking about portfolio balance and the way in which the economy works. Even with a money supply target that was adhered to, and taking the PSBR on board, there would still be the same inflationary effects.[1]

The logic behind this argument is simple. If government borrowing raises interest rates and the demand for money varies inversely with the rate of interest, i.e., velocity increases, the price level will not rise even when the money supply is fixed. Research at the London Business School suggests that the PSBR has an independent inflationary effect, although monetary growth is about twice as inflationary as its PSBR counterpart.

Mr Brittan has puzzled us about the differences between a government issue of bonds and a private sector issue. The idea is that, when the private sector issues a bond, it is because of some real decision behind it: that, in the case of an equity issue, there is some plan to issue real capital and that there has not been a nominal shock to the system. There has been a real decision with a financial decision to go with it. When the government issues a bond to finance some transaction, however, there is not necessarily

---

[1] That the PSBR exerts an inflationary effect independent of the money supply has been noted by numerous writers, e.g., J. Tobin and W. Buiter, 'The Long Run Effects of Fiscal and Monetary Policy on Aggregate Demand', in J. Stein (ed.), *Monetarism*, North Holland, Amsterdam, 1976.

a real decision to go with it. It depends what the transaction is. If, for example, a new road system is built which increases real output in the economy, there will be both a financial and a real shock together. If, on the other hand, the government issues bonds, say, to raise the salaries of academics, there will be merely a financial, and hence inflationary, shock.

WILLIAM KEEGAN: I would like to know Professor Minford's view of the behaviour of the German and Japanese economies in similar situations. On Samuel Brittan's point, and on Michael Beenstock's, I would be interested in views on this distinction between bonds for road-building and for other purposes, and on how this analysis would apply, roughly, say, before and after the mid-1970s. Professor Minford did not mention wages, but I have a feeling that, in the discussion of bonds, two attitudes can be held: first, on the world after the inflationary explosion, particularly in the public sector; and, secondly, on the period before then, when we used to think of 'above the line' and 'below the line'.

HAROLD ROSE: Going back to the earlier discussion about private and public sector borrowing, I would like to take further the assumption that Patrick Minford seems to be making, which is that deadweight debt issued by the government will have a financial effect. He is making the assumption, I suppose, that the economy is at or near what may roughly be called a full employment or sustainable employment level and therefore that no increase in output is possible. The question then is whether the government can increase its share of output, if it has good road projects to finance, for example, simply by issuing bonds. It can attract real resources away from the private sector by bond issues only by driving up the real rate of interest. In Patrick Minford's model, the government cannot drive up the real rate of interest because Britain is only a small part of the world economy.

ANTHONY COURAKIS: I understood Patrick Minford to emphasise the importance of the PSBR, or the government's deficit; so I do not see that Michael Beenstock's argument on the *kind* of expenditure has any direct bearing on the issues. At the same time, and as Sam Brittan's question also suggests, Patrick Minford has not offered us any clear indication on how exactly the PSBR or the government's deficit affects private expenditures and expectations of inflation, as he claims it does. I think, however, that what he had in mind was something along these lines: there is an increased government deficit; people come to associate it with a future increase in the rate of growth of the money supply, irrespective of how the deficit might be financed in the short run; and it is only insofar as people form such expectations that the deficit has an effect on the expected rate of inflation and therefore the rest of the effects that Patrick Minford described. It is not that changes in the stock of government bonds, which may result from this deficit, have an inflationary effect; it is the fact that an increase in the government's deficit results in a higher expected rate of increase in the money supply. It is therefore the higher expected rate of increase in the money supply that produces the subsequent inflationary effects.

This is, of course, consistent with some schools of thought. It is also perfectly consistent with Patrick Minford's results which derive from a period during which the government did pursue a particular policy towards nominal interest rates which implied a closer relationship between the PSBR or government deficit and the rate of increase in the money supply than would otherwise have ensued. In the event, what the estimates pick up to some extent is not a government financing requirement effect on expenditures, but the effect that the government's deficit has on people's anticipations about the rate of increase in the money supply. Sam Brittan's argument would then be perfectly valid despite Patrick Minford's results, because what the results pick up is not a situation in which government deficits financed through the sale of bonds cause an increase in the anticipated rate of inflation, but rather one where, even when the deficit is for a time financed through sales of bonds, it still causes anticipations of a higher rate of increase in the money supply and this in turn results in higher expected inflation.

ALAN BUDD: I disagree with what Anthony Courakis has said, but I am sure that Patrick Minford is quite capable of dealing with that in due course. Certainly there could be a direct effect on prices simply through a shift in portfolios. Prices would rise because of an excess supply of financial assets.

I want to comment on Harold Rose's argument about the extent to which the government, when issuing debt, may or may not be able to attract resources to itself. It seems to me reasonable to assume that the public sector will always get all the resources it wants, in one way or another. If it does not do so through some market real rate of interest, it will eventually do so through inflation, or through taxation. One way it can get real resources in the shorter term is when an increase in the deficit induces people to anticipate not necessarily a subsequent increase in the money supply but in taxation. They instantly recognise that any issue of government debt which appears to have an effect on wealth will have an immediately offsetting wealth effect in the form of a tax liability to finance future interest payments. Total wealth, therefore, is unchanged and in that way the personal sector acts to offset the increase in public expenditure. But there will be an increase in financial assets which could have an inflationary effect.

MORRIS PERLMAN: I would like to comment on the difference, if any, between private and government creation of debt. It is usually said that private creation of debt crowds out other types of private creation of debt and therefore the total asset portfolio remains unchanged. In his analysis of the wealth effect of the government's policy, Professor Minford allows some crowding out in the goods sector but not in the portfolio sector; that is, the rising interest rate also crowds out private debt. Let me also add to Alan Budd's point about anticipation of future tax changes. Within a model of rational expectations, which Professor Minford uses, if tax changes are taken into account the whole wealth effect—the portfolio effect—disappears too. And therefore to attribute some of the expenditure changes to the pure wealth portfolio effect is problematic within a rational expectations model where these future tax changes on the debt would be anticipated.

One point not directly related but which Professor Minford mentioned in his paper should be raised. I am an old-style Chicago monetarist and it is therefore money I am worried about. I believe that most of the mileage in this model derives from the increase in money which is associated with the PSBR. It is therefore important to see why an increase in the PSBR must be associated with the change in the quantity of money. And although Professor Minford does acknowledge that similar results are obtained even if the PSBR is not associated with any growth in the money supply, those results arise from the wealth effect, not the portfolio effect.

TIM CONGDON: The explanation of why an increase in the PSBR causes higher inflation, which is implicit in what Patrick Minford has been saying, is that, with a budget deficit and no rise in nominal income, the ratio of the stock of nominal financial assets (including government bonds in particular) to income is rising. The idea is that this ratio cannot rise indefinitely. To bring it back to equilibrium, nominal income has to rise. As real income is fixed by supply factors, there has to be inflation.

There are several difficulties with that argument, and one is obvious. If the rate of interest rises, the market value of the debt declines. The ratio of the market value of the debt to income has not increased. It follows that an increase in the PSBR accompanied by higher interest rates may not lead to extra inflation. There is a difficulty, then, in knowing what is the right ratio to follow—the market value or nominal value of debt to income. The point, of course, is that interest rate changes do not affect the nominal value of the debt.

There is an additional problem which has been ventilated in a number of comments. The ratio of nominal debt to national income need not increase if the extra public debt crowds out private debt. This raises a very interesting question. Most discussions of crowding out are expressed in flow terms. Attention is focussed on the effect on other spending decisions in the year when extra public spending is pushed into the economy, not on the permanent effect on the total array of financial assets. In other words, the debt-to-income ratio arguments are a shift towards expressing crowding out in stock terms.

The point I want to emphasise is that it does not follow, merely because there is a budget deficit and the ratio of nominal debt to income is rising, that the ratio of the market value of the debt to income is also rising, since an increase in the rate of interest could actually reduce it.

BRITTAN: Anthony Courakis took my point much further than I would have done. Like the Bank of England, I am not quite sure what money is, and I am quite prepared to accept that a much wider range of financial assets than M3 affects the price level. I simply raised the question of what makes the government unique. This very necessary discussion then followed about what exactly the government is doing with the finance it is raising, and William Keegan asked whether 'below' and 'above the line' should be redefined in some meaningful way.

ARTHUR SELDON: Why cannot we think about money as something that, as I like all economists was taught, can be used in exchange for goods and services? If it can be defined as purchasing power in any form, then it is money.

RUSSELL LEWIS: If the answer, ultimately, for getting rid of the PSBR is to borrow indexed short-term bonds, why not go the whole hog and borrow the whole of the PSBR on short-term bonds? What would be the effect of that? Would this deny the private sector resources on an enormous scale? Or, since we are now into a free market in exchange rates, since exchange control has now gone, would it mean an enormous increase in Arab money coming into the country, and what difference would that make?

COURAKIS: There was no suggestion in what I said earlier that the PSBR is unimportant. Rather that the way the deficit is financed is also very important. In Patrick Minford's analysis at least, there was no explanation, or even indication, of how, or why, the way in which the PSBR is financed can be disregarded (as he does). Undoubtedly portfolio effects are important. But, granted this, the shift to saying that the focus should be entirely on the PSBR, forgetting the way in which this requirement is financed, is too extreme.

MINFORD: Let me try to clarify what I am saying. I assume that the private sector balance sheet is consolidated and that the private sector acts as if this is so. This assumption (perhaps an extreme one) implies that the difference between private sector debt and public sector debt is that the latter constitutes assets of the private sector but not liabilities of it—except in the indirect sense that, in the future, government will have to service them by appropriate changes in taxation.

Morris Perlman's point is that public sector debt is not net wealth for private agents because they will discount these future tax liabilities. I am not, however, emphasising that this debt is net wealth, though it could be. The issue here is that of portfolio balance. An increase in the PSBR, financed by money or not, will give rise to the acquisition by private agents of nominal debt which, though balanced formally by future tax liabilities, will nevertheless not represent a desired balance in their portfolios between financial assets, money and goods. They therefore attempt to shift their portfolio composition back towards the desired balance, by adjusting their spending and by swapping bonds for money. Tax liabilities may affect this balance but they are not perfect substitutes for the debt that has been issued.

It is conceivable that intermediaries would spring up to mediate the tax liabilities and provide the private sector with such a perfect substitute. I assume that this does not take place, for example because of the difficulties of marketing tax liabilities. This is admittedly an institutional restriction which, however, appears to be generally applicable—as applicable as the other important institutional fact that currency carries no interest.

Let me expand further on the issue of where the line is to be drawn between public and private sector financing. Different countries have different institutional set-ups; the definitions of private and public sectors are different. Estimated relationships between private sector holdings of financial assets and their stock of goods are correspondingly different. If large and successful parts of the private sector (such as ICI) became part of the nationalised sector, this would lead to new 'private sector' portfolio relationships. It might reasonably be expected in this case that they would shift in such a way as to permit a higher PSBR for given monetary growth and inflation rates.

PSBR and monetary growth

I confirm Anthony Courakis's interpretation of my argument that a rise in the PSBR leads over some time-scale to complementary rises in monetary growth. To hold down monetary growth indefinitely would imply, in a closed economy, an indefinite increase in real interest rates. In an open economy the situation is different, because the government may borrow from abroad. There is, however, no great difference in principle from the closed economy case. As the stock of debt in overseas hands continuously increases relative to other assets, foreign lenders will require continuously increasing real returns to absorb it. We are familiar enough with such cases from the recent history of Euro-market financing.

There is the important and obvious exception to this rule that, where a government is funding a project with a commercial return the cash flow from which will be contractually directed to servicing the loan, finance can be raised against this collateral at standard market rates for as long as the project continues. But to define this exception highlights the usual case of governments borrowing for general expenditure which will generate no recoverable stream of revenue.

CONGDON: Could you explain sustained inflation where the government was also running a sustained budget surplus? There are certain historical examples of that.

MINFORD: It is feasible, in principle. The private sector would have to be running a financial deficit (i.e., investing more than it is saving), which is unusual but clearly possible.

2. The Monetary Base Question

HAROLD ROSE

London Graduate School of Business Studies and
Barclays Bank Limited

The Author

HAROLD ROSE is Esmée Fairbairn Visiting Professor of Finance, London Graduate School of Business Studies, and Group Economic Adviser to Barclays Bank since 1975. He was educated at Davenant Foundations School and the London School of Economics and Political Science. From 1948-58 he was head of the Economic Intelligence Department of the Prudential Assurance Company. He was Director of Studies to the Course in Industrial Financing, London School of Economics, 1958-63; Reader in Economics, University of London, 1963-65; Esmée Fairbairn Professor of Finance, London Graduate School of Business Studies, 1965-75. Author of *The Economic Background to Investment* (1960); *Management Education in the 1970s: Growth and Issues* (1969). For the IEA he wrote *Disclosure in Company Accounts* (Eaton Paper 1, 1963, second edition, 1965) and a Commentary to *Choice in Currency* (Occasional Paper 48, 1976). He is a member of the IEA's Advisory Council.

I. THREE BASIC ISSUES

There are three basic issues involved in the question of whether we should change the technique of monetary control from the existing reserve asset system to a monetary base system:

First, there is the perennial conflict between controlling price and controlling quantity; between controlling interest rates and controlling the quantity of money, accepting the consequences for interest rates.

Second, within that, there is the question of whether it is desirable to have some degree of control over short-term rates of interest in particular.

Third, there is the question of what sort of technique is likely to be most *predictable* in its effect on the quantity of money.

Failure of the 'corset'

I am going to assume that none of you wants monetary policy based on administrative devices such as the 'corset'. The corset has been ineffective as well as unfair, and it will be dropped some time this year. So I do not want to discuss what are essentially side-issues concerning the corset, and neither do I want to discuss particular technical problems such as whether to have gilt-edged issues by tender rather than sales through the 'tap'; although I would say that the fact that the reserve asset system has had to be supplemented by devices such as the corset seems to me to suggest that something is wrong. It may be, of course, that the only thing that is wrong with the present thrust of monetary policy is the size of the PSBR and the unwillingness of the authorities to accept the interest-rate implications of their fiscal policy. Even if this were true, it would leave unresolved the question of whether monetary policy might be more effective if the authorities adopted a different set of techniques.

II. MONETARY CONTROL—FROM RESERVE ASSETS
TO CASH BALANCES

The main change that would be required to shift to a monetary base system—and I am not going to get involved in discussions of whether notes and coin in the hand of the banks should be included—would be the replacement of the existing spectrum of reserve assets as the pivot of control by the balances of the banks with the Bank of England. I assume that the banks would be required to hold a minimum ratio of balances to deposits with the Bank of England.

Restricting the Bank's role as lender-of-last-resort

To make such a system of control effective, the Bank of England would have to end the practice it has followed since the 19th century of *always* acting as a lender-of-last-resort to provide the 'cash', i.e. balances with the central bank, which the banks need to support a given level of deposits. We do have a 'cash' ratio within the existing reserve asset spectrum; but it is ineffective, because the authorities will always provide whatever cash is needed to support the level of deposits that emerges. That is, they fit cash to deposits and make no attempt to limit the supply of cash in order to control the deposit total except by altering at intervals the interest rate at which they will supply cash, so that the present cash ratio system is primarily a means of controlling short-term rates. Under a classic monetary-base or cash-ratio control system, the Bank of England would have to place some restriction on the size of its lender-of-last-resort facilities to individual banks, as in the USA and Germany, except at times of crisis.

The system developed in Britain, which seems to be the only large country in the world to have a wide reserve asset spectrum as opposed to a narrow cash-ratio type of control, is partly the result of the increase in the size of the floating debt in the First World War. If one reads the inquiries into monetary policy in the early 1920s one finds something said which is echoed again in the Radcliffe Report of 1959, namely a pre-occupation on the part of the authorities with financing the floating debt as the justification for having *continuous and automatic* lender-of-last-resort facilities. The justification offered was that without these facilities the authorities would lose control of the floating debt, in that the market would not be prepared to hold the floating debt, which would therefore be monetised. This is analogous with the sort of argument we heard made by the authorities in the 1950s and 1960s for the case for always supporting the bond market.

The other point one should notice is that the government never really had a money supply policy until the late 1960s. One hardly finds the quantity of money mentioned in Treasury and Bank of England papers before the 1960s. Policy was aimed instead at the flow of 'credit' and the level of interest rates; the traditional official view of concentrating on interest-rate policy as being the object of policy rather than money supply therefore underlies the long-standing aversion to a monetary base system.

Disadvantages of reserve asset system

The difficulty about the reserve asset system is that the authorities need to have a wide range of 'information', a wide set, as it were, of simultaneous equations about demand and supply conditions concerning the whole spectrum of reserve assets. It has to have a set of equations about the effect of interest rates on the demand for advances and the effect of interest-rate policy on the private sector's willingness to take up government bonds, for example, in a situation in which nominal interest rates are not in practice very good guides because of the importance of inflationary expectations which are not directly identifiable.

The reserve asset system is not operated, it should be noted, in the way in which some textbooks used to say it worked. I was brought up on the view of the system in which the central bank determined the level of the reserve assets and the banks then adjusted to that level, i.e. on some basis of a deposit multiplier. The Bank of England does not operate in that sort of fashion. The importance of the reserve asset system to the Bank of England is not primarily through any deposit multiplier effect, but in creating a framework enabling the authorities to have control over interest rates. It is through this manipulation of interest rates that the authorities see themselves as controlling the quantity of money.

The basic arguments against this system are that the range of assets in the control mechanism is too wide and that there is an elasticity of supply of these assets on the part of the non-bank sector. The result is that the supply of these assets to the banks is not fully under the control of the Bank of England.

A subsidiary objection is that the existing reserve asset system forces the authorities to conduct their open-market policy largely at the long-term end of the gilt-edged market. There is one advantage of this method which I am prepared to concede, namely that the distinction between long-term bonds and 'money' is clearer than that between short-term paper and 'money'. By operating at the long-term end of the market, the authorities are at least creating assets which are not close substitutes for the monetary aggregates. The disadvantage is that operations in the long-term market are most difficult to judge correctly in terms of the interest elasticity of the non-bank demand for government bonds, especially bearing in mind that the only rates which the authorities can observe are nominal rates, not real rates.

III. ARGUMENTS FOR A MONETARY BASE SYSTEM

The arguments in favour of a monetary base system in which, to simplify, there is only one reserve asset, namely balances with the Bank of England, are these:

1. The supply of that asset to the banking system is under the direct control of the central bank. The central bank, by altering the shape of its own balance sheet, must affect the supply of that asset.

2. *Any* asset which the central bank sells,[1] and not only long-term bonds, would affect the cash reserves of the bank. By contrast, if the central bank sells Treasury bills under the present system, there are two problems. First, even if those Treasury bills are sold to the non-bank sector, there is a potential stock of reserve assets on which the banks can draw if it is profitable for them to do so. Secondly, if the authorities sell Treasury bills to the banking sector, the Bank of England always provides the cash to enable the banking sector to take up those bills, so that there is no restrictive effect on money supply.

Treasury bill issue 'creates short-term liquidity on demand'

The Bank of England put the case for this system to the Radcliffe Committee in a curious way. It said that we needed to have the discount houses underwrite the Treasury bill issue and that, in order for the discount houses, which are almost 100 per cent geared institutions, to be willing to do this, they must have automatic lender-of-last-resort facilities. All that statement means, however, is that, insofar as lender-of-last-resort facilities are implemented, the Bank of England itself is really taking up the Treasury bills the Treasury is issuing, so that what you have in reality is an engine that

---

[1] Including sales to the banks themselves.

creates short-term liquidity more or less on demand. The authorities control short-term interest rates, but the general effect is to create liquidity in the money market which has to be offset by the sale of bonds in the long-term gilt-edged market.

A monetary base system would not require the authorities to consider such a wide range of equations to control the money supply. In the extreme case, if the banks were to maintain constant cash reserve ratios, if the Bank of England could always control the structure of its own balance sheet, it would be able to achieve whatever money supply target it set. The classic argument against that proposition, which the Bank of England has always been inclined to give, is that if it were to attempt to fix the level of cash reserves from week to week and possibly even from month to month, the effect would be to magnify short-term interest-rate fluctuations very considerably.

Risks and costs of short-term interest rate fluctuations

There is undoubtedly a respectable case to be made in favour of the argument that short-term interest-rate fluctuations might be excessive from the point of view of national welfare.

The whole interest-rate spectrum might be much more unstable, and two effects would follow from what would amount to an increase in risk. First, investors would tend to hold shorter-term portfolios than would otherwise be the case; and this might be disadvantageous for borrowers. Secondly, if interest rates as a whole were more unstable, dealers in financial markets would need wider spreads to offset the higher risks they would be facing. Wider spreads would constitute a real cost which has to be borne by society.

The reply to this is that the present system itself creates a high degree of instability of interest rates, not necessarily from week to week, but certainly from quarter to quarter, because of the fact that policy is relatively ineffective in hitting monetary targets. As this tends to cause wide swings in the long-term gilt-edged market, we may get the worst of both worlds, namely a high variance of money supply and a high variance of interest rates.

As for the problem of interest-rate instability under a monetary base system, what is really important is whether instability spreads along the whole maturity spectrum, for all systems can work with an overnight rate that fluctuates widely. It is by no means clear, therefore, that, even if there were—and known to be—wide fluctuations in the overnight rate or seven-day rate, the whole interest-rate spectrum would be as unstable as at present.

The extent to which we would get interest-rate fluctuations, however, would itself depend on whether private sector operators came in to replace the stabilisation function that is now exercised by the central bank. Because the central bank is the most powerful operator in the market and because its actions tend to be in steps, it is very hard for private operators to take the risks of stabilisation under the present system. If we were to move to a more 'hands-off' type of system, private speculators should be willing to absorb some of the shocks the central bank at present sees itself as having to shoulder.

Monetary base system 'desirable'

So I think that a move towards a monetary base system is desirable. It would have other implications, of course. As short-term rates are those which, in the short run at any rate, have the most powerful effect on international capital movements, it also follows that a move to the monetary base would make it all the more imperative to run a freely-floating exchange rate system.

Although I am a supporter of a monetary base system, I would not, however, go as far as some advocates do in the claims that I would make for it or, indeed, for any other monetary control system. Professor Brian Griffiths, for example, seems to think that the authorities could operate in a *completely* hands-off fashion.[2] They would publish a sequence of reserve targets, and would operate so as to keep on target, come what may. The obvious difficulty about such a policy is that the level of reserves, while under the control of the authorities, need not be identical with the reserves desired by the banks in a system in which the banks are subject to uncontrollable changes in deposits through the operation of an overdraft system. It is perhaps part of the story that one reason why some countries other than the UK operate a cash-ratio system is the smaller part played abroad by the classic overdraft, which places the level of deposits under the control of the banks' customers in the short run.

Would banks demand more excess reserves?

One possible result of a monetary base system, therefore, is that the banks might want to hold more excess reserves, which would intro-

---

[2] 'The reform of monetary control in the UK', City University's *Annual Monetary Review*, No. 1, October 1979.

duce a degree of uncertainty into the effectiveness of official policy. The variability of reserve ratios would probably be more than exists at present, when the commercial banks keep their reserve assets only a little above the required minimum. A cash-ratio system in which the authorities were not always going to bail them out would be one to which, for reasons of commercial prudence, the banks would be bound to react by having excess reserves that varied from time to time.

If so, that might confront the central bank with the problem of predicting bank behaviour similar to that which it has at present. However, the Swiss central bank, for example, certainly does operate a reasonably effective money supply, despite the fact that it does not prescribe a required reserve ratio on the part of the banks and that the cash ratios actually held by the banks do vary from time to time. Moreover, the absence of large excess reserves in today's situation may be more apparent than real if a potential supply of reserve assets exists *outside* the banking system for the banks to acquire.

Balance-sheet control by the Bank

Another example of possible slippage is that, although it is true that the Bank of England, by adjusting its own balance sheet, can alter the level of bank reserves, the Bank of England's own balance sheet may not be as much under its own control as it is sometimes assumed. If the banks are short of reserves, for example, they will bid for them in the inter-bank market, where rates would rise. This could lead non-banks, for example, to let their Treasury bills run down to take up the paper issued by the banks, and the Bank of England would then have the same sort of problem that it has now of whether to allow interest rates to rise or to take these Treasury bills off the market in order to control interest rates and let the level of reserves rise.

The general point I want to emphasise is that the Bank of England would inevitably find itself having to take awkward rate decisions when confronted with money markets in which liquidity was slipping out of its control. We therefore come back to the fundamental question of whether the short-term interest-rate fluctuations that would result would be excessive. Moreover, the more the fluctuations in interest rates, the larger are the excess reserves held by the banks likely to be. These are the joint problems which have to be confronted.

SHORT READING LIST ON MONETARY BASE CONTROL

Congdon, Tim, 'Should Britain adopt monetary base control?', *The Banker,* February 1980.

Foot, M. D. K. W., Goodhart, C. A. E. G. and Hotson, A. C., 'Monetary base control', *Bank of England Quarterly Bulletin,* June 1979.

Griffiths, Professor Brian, 'The reform of monetary control in the UK', City University's *Annual Monetary Review,* No. 1, October 1979.

Rose, Professor Harold, 'Control of the money supply', *Barclays Bank Review,* November 1979.

Savage, David, 'Monetary Targets and the Control of the Money Supply', National Institute of Economic & Social Research, *Economic Review,* No. 89, August 1979.

Questions and Discussion

ARTHUR SELDON (*Chairman*): I think we should not ignore that we are concerned not only with the power of government as a technical device aiming at optimum outcomes, but also with government comprised of politicians with short-term electoral aims. We are in danger of losing sight of these broader and shorter-term aims in discussing the subject as a wholly technical matter of optimum rules. As a bit of an anarchist myself, I would like to see government deprived of the power of being an active and independent agency in monetary management and policy.

JOHN WOOD: One of the difficulties about understanding the controversy of the moment, for someone who has not followed it and is trying to pick it up, is that the terminology has changed completely. I had never heard of 'monetary base' until recently, and 'vault money', too, is an entirely new concept. If we go back a long time, there used to be two ratios, a 10 per cent cash ratio and a 30 per cent liquidity ratio; one was changed to 8 per cent and then the other, because it was a way of stimulating the economy, went to 28 per cent.

ANTHONY COURAKIS: The 10 per cent never coincided with the 30 per cent.

WOOD: That does not matter too much since we are still talking about the choice between two controls in entirely different languages.

HAROLD ROSE: In Britain we have usually discussed the question in terms of controlling the quantity of 'cash'—and by cash is meant commercial bank balances at the Bank of England. In the United States the terminology is slightly different—for reasons that are not important—and it became that of the 'monetary base'. But it is the same issue, namely, whether the Bank of England should make the cash ratio an effective constraint or not.

WOOD: Yes, and there were those at that time, including, I think Manning Dacey, who were trying to insist on that. Do you recall that or not?

ROSE: For many years the discussion centred on which ratio was the effective one. The textbooks used to say that in Britain there was an effective cash ratio system. Then it was pointed out by Dacey and others that, as the banking system could always turn Treasury bills into cash because the Bank of England was always prepared to buy them, the cash ratio was not the effective control. Effective control was really exercised by a wider spectrum of liquid assets from which the present reserve asset system has developed.

WOOD: May I put my final question on Harold Rose's talk? Did I understand him to say that, although he preferred the 'cash ratio' system, he feared that, even with the authorities insisting on variable cash ratios, they still would not have a total hold on the system?

ROSE: Any good undergraduate can invent a system in which the Bank of England has week-by-week control of the money supply. But the fundamental problem is that a system of that sort may amount to trying to operate through a licensing system. It would really be saying to individual banks that they have a licence to do *x* amount this week, so much next week, and so on. The question is what form of monetary control is compatible with running a commercial banking system, as well as what system is compatible with acceptable interest-rate behaviour. Therefore it would be wrong for the authorities to attempt to control the deposits of the banking system on a week-by-week basis. On the other hand, it is clearly too lax for them to control deposits only over a matter of years. Thus there is some point at which there is an optimum trade-off between the need to control the money supply and the flexibility needed to run a banking system at all.

Perhaps I should add that until recently the Bank of England has been rather naughty, because it has appeared to identify a monetary base system with week-by-week control; and it is quite easy to show that week-by-week control of bank deposits would be authoritarian.

MICHAEL BEENSTOCK: I am puzzled by the interest that is emerging in the idea of the monetary base. To rise to the challenge that Arthur Seldon threw down, the entire debate is going to do no end of harm to the revival of interest in financial economics, especially in relation to inflation. Morris Perlman talked about a scheme which, he claimed, any undergraduate could devise: the scheme he suggested recently[1] was prefaced with the admission that he did not know why anyone might want to control it.

My starting point is that, in seeking to control the money supply, it must be specifically M3 that we want to control initially. But I have difficulty getting to this point of departure. Once it has been reached, the issues can be discussed. However, as was made clear in the discussion after Professor Minford's paper (pp. 23-31), economic theory does not suggest any specific level of M as the *sine qua non* for controlling inflation. This depends on the portfolio balance, the whole spectrum of financial assets. It may have been for public relations purposes that, in the journals, in the newspapers and among politicians, M3 was presented as something simple that everyone could understand. We now have to move beyond that. It would be quite misconceived to turn the clock back and say that 'born-again monetarism' amounts to the control of M3. When we set up some new-fangled devices for building this thing we call M3, we will do no more than distract attention from what are the basic issues. That is my first point. I agree with Charles Goodhart that this is an issue on which we should not waste too much time since economic theory never suggested in the first place that this was how to think about it.

Are monetarists making the *dirigiste* mistake?

My second point, which I find something of a contradiction, is that there has been a vague suggestion of some connection between the rise of monetarism and the rôle of the market, in that monetarists by and large believe in allowing market forces freedom to work in their own way. When, in days past, we considered that the unions played a large part in causing inflation, and that international cor-

---

[1] 'The Cash Reserve System', paper presented to the Money Study Group at the London School of Economics, December 1979.

porations set their own prices, the way was opened for a whole era of *dirigisme*—with incomes policies and price controls—in order to tackle the problems directly.

The 'born-again monetarists' are making the same mistake now, inasmuch as they have discovered M3 and wonder how they should go about controlling it. Instead of leaving financial markets to work in their own way (and, although they may suffer from some random fluctuations, they do exhibit basic trends), they claim that M3 must be controlled in the same *dirigiste* manner that is exactly counter to free-market philosophy. Instead of a Price Commission there might have to be a Money Supply Commission, with all the bureaucratic devices required to set up norms and rules with which to control M3. Even if it was the case that economic theory suggested M3 to be the *sine qua non* for the long-run control of inflation, it does not follow automatically that M3 Commissions should be set up to devise methods of controlling M3 in the short run and that all we can hope for from government—insofar as it has an important bearing on the supply of financial assets—is that it should make its position clear (in the way that Alan Budd and others[2] have suggested) through a financial plan, as a counterpart of decisions on public expenditure. Markets would then react accordingly. This short-term obsession with M3 is quite absurd.

SAMUEL BRITTAN: Towards the end of his remarks Michael Beenstock said something that worried me. He gave the impression that raising MLR to 17 per cent was a mistake, for nothing needed to be done. But if the whole spectrum of financial assets is considered, and not M3 alone, it is clear that this policy was more inflationary than intended. What then would Dr Beenstock do? Would he simply adopt a PSBR policy and sit back? If he would suggest something more than that, perhaps he could give details.

MORRIS PERLMAN: When I said that we do not need to discuss why we want to control M3, I did not mean that we do not know why we want to control it. I disagree strongly with the general viewpoint expressed by Michael Beenstock. There is a good reason to separate money from other financial assets, if for no other reason than that discussed in the previous paper. In a world of perfect rational expectations, money is not like the PSBR, like debt. Money

---

[2] Alan Budd, 'Monetary Targets and a Financial Plan', *Economic Outlook,* November 1979 (Gower Publishing, Farnborough).

creation is like dropping wealth from heaven. In terms of wealth effects, any issue of government debt, with perfect foresight and perfect discounting of future taxes, and no constraints, is a non-event.

Money is thus quite a different kind of asset. Now whether M2 or M3 or M27 is money is a problem. But this is a theoretical problem based on the issues of 'inside money', 'outside money', and whether 'inside money' is wealth or not.

The financial structure—the structure of assets in the economy—is obviously important too. There are all sorts of substitution effects going on, and so there might be other kinds of effects from an issue of public sector debt and the kind of debt structure determined by government, in terms of general substitution effects in portfolios. But in terms of wealth effects, which, to some extent, all monetarists from Hume and Ricardo onwards had in mind, this kind of distinction is crucial.

Returning to the question, which I know to be of great theoretical interest, of financial and portfolio structures is in some sense returning to the Radcliffe Report—to the idea of controlling liquidity and credit in the economy. If this is the source of interest, then I would suggest that the government stay well clear of it. What the government should do—and I am prepared to go along with Michael Beenstock here—is to warn individuals that it is going to issue so much debt. Just as ICI, or any other private concern, can issue a certain amount of debt which will go into individual portfolios and affect interest rates, so government-issued debt will lead, amongst other things, to changes in relative rates. Some of these effects can be traced. But the reason for the different nature of governmental activity in the provision of money is that government is the only institution in the system that can *create* money. Since this has an inflationary effect, and since government is a monopolist in this activity, it should be controlled.

HAMISH McRAE: I want to make a 'showbiz' observation, as opposed to an economic one, which picks up Michael Beenstock's point. Trying to establish in the public mind that money matters has been a painful, long, and difficult job for communicators. It has taken four or five years or so to achieve it. The concept of sterling M3 has been very useful because it is something which people now understand. Trade unionists now refer to it in their own conversations. I appreciate that there is no necessary link between the move to a monetary base and the move away from sterling M3 as the principal monetary aggregate with which we operate. But in practice it is going to be very difficult to explain to people what is happening if both the system of control and the aggregates that we are trying to control are changed. In other words, as a communicator I do not see how I can go back over everything that has been said for several years to the extent that one aggregate is probably better than most, and start now to try to explain that we must concentrate on something else.

COURAKIS: Professor Rose has quite substantially qualified his statements on the desirability of pursuing a monetary base policy. His view that 'a move towards a monetary base system is desirable' is coloured by an awareness that, at any given point in time, the authorities will have to take a position on interest rates. There is no way the markets can be left to their own devices. The authorities must always be involved because of government debt; they are always involved in their capacity as lender of last resort; and they must decide how much to intervene. From such a viewpoint there is not much difference between a situation in which the monetary base is employed as a means by which to express or summarise policy at any given time, and a circumstance in which, following what Michael Beenstock referred to as 'the Alan Budd position', policy announcements describe more explicitly the *nature* of the strategy followed.

The latter does not, of course, imply that the choice of strategy (and so, too, the choice between policies which aim to secure the particular path of one monetary aggregate as opposed to another) is a matter of indifference.[3] Furthermore, for other reasons than those suggested by Morris Perlman, there are strong theoretical grounds for distinguishing between alternative financial assets, and that portfolio analysis—though it affords the opportunity to write a system of equations that describes choices between alternative assets—does anything but provide a *rationale* for failing to distinguish between financial assets.

Control of bank deposits: the quantity/price trade-off

Focussing on the main issue, however, namely, how more determinate

---

[3] This issue is discussed at further length in A. S. Courakis, 'Monetary Targets: Alternative Interpretations and Appraisal of recent US, UK and German Policies', in A. S. Courakis (ed.), *Inflation, Depression and Economic Policy in the West,* Mansell, London, 1980.

control of bank deposits in the UK can be attained, though I find myself in broad sympathy with many of the points that Professor Rose reminded us of, I would place the emphasis quite differently. Noting the three issues mentioned at the beginning of Professor Rose's paper, let us focus on the question of trade-off between quantity and price. In this context it is, of course, well established that variations in interest rates comprise a *necessary* condition for control of the money supply, But my interpretation of experience, and of the literature,[4] suggests there is considerable dispute about whether such variations comprise a *sufficient* condition.

There are two ways of viewing these issues. The first is to focus on the demand for money to establish whether and to what extent changes in interest rates bring about changes in the demand for money and correspondingly in the rate of monetary expansion. From this perspective the control of the money supply, it has been suggested,

> 'is achieved by manipulating the interest rate by sliding up and down the demand function for money.'[5]

Obviously in this context the stability of the demand-for-money function is important. And, as Charles Goodhart has noted,[6] the fact that econometric evidence at the beginning of the 1970s tended to suggest 'a stable interest-sensitive demand-for-money function' was an important contributory factor to the 1971 reform and the expressed intention to place more emphasis on variations in interest rates and gilt-edged prices. But, even so, the disillusionment that was soon to follow must not be forgotten.

The earlier Bank of England studies of course rested on a variety of implicit assumptions that could hardly be said to be valid *a priori*

---

[4] For example, A. S. Courakis, 'Monetary Policy: Old Wisdom Behind a New Facade', *Economica,* Vol. XL, No. 157, February 1973, pp. 73-86, and the Bank's recent description of 'The Gilt-Edged Market', *Bank of England Quarterly Bulletin,* June 1979.

[5] M. J. Parkin, 'A Comparison of Alternative Techniques of Monetary Control under Rational Expectations', *Manchester School,* Vol. 46, No. 3, September 1978, pp. 252-87; also J. L. Pierce and T. D. Thomson, 'Some Issues in Controlling the Stock of Money', in Federal Reserve Bank of Boston, *Controlling Monetary Aggregates II: The Implementation,* FRBB, Boston, September 1972.

[6] C. A. E. Goodhart, 'Bank of England Studies of the Demand for Money Function', in F. Masera *et al.* (eds.), *Econometric Research in European Central Banks,* Banca d'Italia, 1975; and 'Problems of Monetary Management: the UK Experience', in A. S. Courakis (ed.), *op. cit.*

in the conditions of the 1970s.[7] Furthermore, the later studies also exhibited a variety of conceptual weaknesses.[8] But the fact remains that to this day no demand function for M3 (or sterling M3) has been traced for the UK that is sufficiently robust (on a quarterly basis) to constitute a reliable foundation for policy design.

However, apart from the failure to trace a stable demand-for-money function for what the authorities, at least, regard as the 'relevant' monetary aggregate, there has been a feeling that attempting to secure stable and steady monetary growth in the short run carries with it the risk of instrument instability, in that interest rates will need to fluctuate increasingly widely.[9] Whether or not this is so depends on the values of the parameters of the relationship between interest rates and the money stock.[10] But, *a priori,* the possibility cannot be excluded that, even when the demand for money is known with reasonable accuracy, the continuous attainment of desired values for the monetary aggregate considered to be the target for policy will require successively larger movements in interest rates.

Reduction in the rate of growth of reserve assets

So much for the case of control of monetary aggregates perceived in terms of the demand-for-money function. The alternative way of viewing the *necessary* versus *sufficient* issue is through tracing the process set in motion by a reduction in bank reserves—or, more realistically in a growing setting, by a downward deviation in the rate of growth of reserves. If banks are thus made short of reserves they will *individually* attempt to increase their reserve holdings either by decumulating non-reserve assets or (barring 'corsets' and ceilings on rates paid on deposits) by bidding more actively for deposits. In either case, of course, provided that we assume the authorities do not

---

[7] For example, A. S. Courakis, 'Serial Correlation and a Bank of England Study of the Demand for Money', *Economic Journal,* Vol. 88, September 1978, pp. 537-48.

[8] *Ibid.* Also M. J. Artis and M. Lewis, 'The Demand for Money in the United Kingdom', *Manchester School,* Vol. 43, No. 2, June 1976, pp. 147-81.

[9] For example, L. A. Dicks-Mireaux, 'British Monetary Experience 1973-77', paper presented to the Eighth Konstanz Seminar on Monetary Theory and Monetary Policy, 8-10 June 1977, p. 20.

[10] For example, W. R. White, *The Demand for Money in Canada and the Control of Monetary Aggregates: Evidence from Monthly Data,* Bank of Canada, Staff Research Studies, No. 12, 1978.

intervene, the extent to which the banking sector as a whole can replenish its reserves depends on the elasticities of substitution characterising the public's preferences as between the assets (or liabilities) that the banks offer and those which are eligible as reserve assets. But, even so, there are still a number of possibilities.

The textbook case of multiple contraction in deposits relates to a circumstance in which banks, responding by, say, selling gilts, secure a reduction in deposits but fail to increase their reserves to the desired level. The process continues until interest rates rise to such levels and deposits fall sufficiently to induce both the banks and the public to hold the existing stock of gilt-edged securities together with a smaller volume of monetary liabilities of the government and/or other assets eligible for bank reserves and a smaller volume of deposits.

Suppose, however, that the public recognises that the banking collectivity cannot, by selling gilt-edged securities, make up the reserve deficiency created by, say, special deposits and thus anticipates the *recurrence* of gilt sales by banks. It is then possible that offers of gilt-edged securities by the banks will meet a cool reception, since they combine with the expectation of further sales by the banks. Consequently, it is possible that transactions in the required volume will not be effected and multiple contraction of deposits will not ensue until rates rise to such levels as are deemed by the public to warrant an increase in their holdings of gilt-edged securities commensurate with the decrease in bank assets and liabilities that will ensure equilibrium in bank portfolios. Although it may seem unreasonable to impute to the banks and to the public enough knowledge for such an equilibrium to emerge instantaneously, it can be expected to emerge in time.

Hence, in a setting where the authorities—having caused a reserve deficiency—abstain from any further transactions, the lack of instantaneous adjustment need not frustrate their ability to achieve the multiple contraction of deposits aimed for—whatever gyrations in interest rates the process of adjustment may involve. Yet in practice, even if the continuous need to finance government deficits is disregarded, it must at least be recognised that, in the interval required to identify the equilibrium vector of rates, there is maturing debt to be refinanced—with obvious consequences for the supply of reserves and deposits if the public abstains from taking up new debt.

This kind of scenario, pointing to *uncertainty* as distinct from *risk* (and which I at least find more incisive than the rather vacuous, ultra-formalistic expressions couched in terms of short-run extrapolative expectations about gilt-edged prices), may account for the pessimism so often expressed by the authorities concerning their ability to control monetary (or credit) aggregates by open market operations; and for their expectations that the likely consequence of any such attempt will be large movements in interest rates with little predictable effect on the volume of deposits and credit—at least in the short run. It lends substance to a choice-set (for the authorities) which, unlike the textbook choice between control of interest rates or money supply, does not in the short run compromise the alternatives of price and quantity variations, but rather those of constrained variation in both and creation of conditions which preclude a trade-off.

Determinacy of behavioural relationships in the market

There can, of course, be no doubt that the precise characteristics of behaviour in the gilt-edged market are intimately related to the institutional structure, including the strategy—or customary practices —of the authorities in dealing in this market. I am much less convinced that the so-called 'instability' in the market is the outcome of the authorities' own attempts to prevent sharp fluctuations in gilt-edged prices; and I am certain that econometric evidence has contributed next to nothing on this issue. Indeed, insofar as the problem arises from uncertainty as distinct from risk, from ignorance, from (if preferred) a missing equation in the rational expectations models of operators in this market, it seems to me a problem thoroughly unsuited to conventional econometric treatment. But at any rate (and I wish to stress this emphatically) our perception of the desirability or otherwise of a particular alternative to existing arrangements must be viewed in terms of the extent to which it increases the determinacy of the behavioural relationships through which the authorities' control of instruments of policy (i.e., the discount rate, special deposits, bid and ask prices announced by the government broker *or* quantities of securities of different maturities offered for sale) operates to secure desired values of variables such as M3 or £M3.

From this viewpoint, the issue is not 'the number of equations' that the authorities have to consider to apply policy, nor the economy with regard to 'the number' of equations that control through 'cash ratios' rather than 'reserve asset ratios' is alleged to imply. At any rate, let me record my dissent from what is often presented (and in Professor Rose's paper is adopted) as the self-evident truth that a move to cash ratio and monetary base control dispenses with 'the difficulty' inherent in the present reserve asset system, namely 'that the monetary authority needs to have a wide range of "information", a wide set, as it were, of simultaneous equations about demand and supply conditions on the whole spectrum of reserve assets. It has to have a set of equations about the effects of interest rates on the demand for advances and the effect of interest rate policy on the private sector's willingness to take up government bonds'. For control through cash implies no reduction in the number of equations, since knowledge of the same substitution relationships is required in order to secure control of the monetary base (for any given size of the government's financing requirement) and to assess the implications this would have for the volume of deposits. If these equations (in the sense of means and variances of the parameters pertaining to responses of the banks and the public) are known, our comparison of alternative reserve ratios and of strategies exploiting such ratios must focus on the extent to which competing alternatives to existing arrangements improve the trade-off between the objectives in the authorities' preference function. If these equations are known and the objective is to minimise the variance in the money stock from some targeted value or rate of growth (this being the proximate target defined in attaining some higher-level goal, such as a reduction in inflation), the exercise is indeed straightforward, providing it is assumed that the nature of the relationships is invariant to changes in régime. But when, as seems more pertinent to UK circumstances, the policymaker perceives an environment reminiscent of passages of the Radcliffe Report, the relevant question seems to me to concern the implications of alternative strategies and/or discretionary changes in the structure for reducing the uncertainty the environment presents.

Are interest rate/gilt-edged price variations sufficient?

On the issue of sufficiency of variations in interest rates/gilt-edged prices, we may focus on two groups of changes. The first relates to the *way* in which the authorities operate in the market and the range of instruments offered; the second concerns the *structure of controls* bearing on the clearing banks.

At present, as in the past, the authorities' behaviour is characterised by a willingness to deal continuously 'at prices close to those determined by the general body of transactions in the market'.[11] Furthermore,

> 'the terms of new issues . . . are pitched so as to offer yields very close to those prevailing in the market at the time of the announcement of the issue.'[12]

Neither of these statements implies the pegging of gilt-edged prices. Rather, the Bank's policy amounts to managed flexibility to avoid sharp fluctuations in prices that, in its opinion, would increase uncertainty in the short run and make investors unwilling to take up new stock for maturing stock.

At the same time, this policy of 'leaning into the wind' leaves open the question of the intensity with which the authorities will lean into the wind—implying that the market's expectations are dominated by anticipations of what the authorities' stance in the market will be. The same, of course, would be true if more flexibility in some sense were allowed. Nor is there any difference between the present case, in which the authorities set the terms at which they are prepared to trade, and a circumstance where they announce the quantity and let the market determine the price (as in a tender arrangement). In both cases the relevant piece of information is missing—in the former, the price at which the authorities will deal; in the latter, the quantity they will offer. This would not be so only in the case of a steady pre-determined flow of new issues—which, of course, can *never* coincide with a steady rate of increase in the money supply, however the latter is defined.

The gilt-edged predicament—are less uncertain instruments available?

The alternative is to search for new instruments that are, in some sense, less subject to uncertainty than the standard gilt-edged stock. Efforts in this direction (in the form of partly-paid stocks, convertible stocks and variable-rate stocks) have not been absent in recent years. And, as the Bank of England recently noted,[13] some pattern of higher demand for 'variable-rate stocks', for example, in periods 'when the

---

[11] 'The Gilt Edged Market', *op. cit.*

[12] *Ibid.*

[13] *Ibid.*

outlook for interest rates seemed particularly uncertain and when official sales of conventional stocks were depressed' is clearly discernible. On reflection, however, it can be argued that the intensity of the gilt-edged predicament is not independent of the fact that monetary management under the present definition of bank reserves necessarily implies and is synonymous with transactions in gilt-edged stock of more than a year to maturity and hence wider margins for capital losses or gains than those envisaged as attaching, for the same time interval, to Treasury Bills. In this respect a move to a cash ratio—or even to the complete abolition of compulsory reserve ratios (if the government was willing to forego the tax benefits afforded it by the present system and also by an appropriately chosen system of compulsory cash ratios)—provides the opportunity to conduct open market operations by transacting in Treasury Bills. Banks will then respond to shortages of reserves by selling Treasury Bills, and thus avoid causing expectations of capital losses in gilt-edged of the magnitude implied under present arrangements by sales of gilt-edged (in the absence of an accommodating policy by the Bank of England).

As is true of liquidity ratios, this alternative does imply variations in interest rates as a *necessary* condition for control of the money supply. But (except perhaps insofar as the authorities' behaviour and 'loopholes' in the present definition of reserve ratios offset some of the 'potential instability') it can be argued that it comes closer to rendering such variation a *sufficient* condition. Of course, the obverse side of the coin is greater substitutability with Treasury Bills in the public's demand for money. But this will seem a fair price to pay if it ensures more predictability in the control of, and the demand for, monetary aggregates.

PATRICK MINFORD: We cannot do without monetary targets, at least in our current monetary system. There is not an infinite elasticity of substitution between money and other assets. We have recently had some evidence of a shift in demand for money functions apparently reflecting rapid developments in intermediation. These have given us cause to qualify the view that the interest elasticity is as low as emerged from most studies up to a few years ago. But, assuming that there is in the short term a fair degree of fixity in institutional methods of handling payments that lead to quite a low substitutability between money and other assets, money has an important rôle. Success in controlling money in the short run will be an important short-term influence on prices. Longer-term PSBR control is fundamental because the PSBR regulates the expansion of all financial assets, not merely money. It also follows that PSBR control will avoid the growth of intermediation designed to evade control of some particular definition of money.

Short-term monetary control has another function, related to the government's own decision-making. The PSBR is a lagging indicator and is hard to interpret until months after it is known. Action to correct it is correspondingly easy to postpone. The monetary statistics, for all their faults, are up-to-date and relatively easy to interpret. If the government is committed to monetary targets, corrective action is forced at an early stage when monetary growth accelerates. Interest rates rise first and this in turn forces an early re-appraisal of government finances.

Given the wish to maintain short-term monetary control, the objective is to control the whole spectrum of money and not merely one definition. The advantage of the monetary base method is that it operates on all definitions of money indirectly in a neutral manner, so getting away from the distortions caused by such methods as the 'corset'. M3 could nevertheless be maintained as a target for a transitional period; and it would continue indefinitely to serve as one indicator of monetary growth, relevant to the setting of the monetary base growth rate. However, once experience had been obtained with the new system, monetary targets could be set solely in terms of the monetary base.

ALAN BUDD: I should like to comment on the English vice of the stylised fact and the stylised theory. Professor Minford started his contribution by saying that we needed them. We suffered for 30 years from one set of stylised theories, namely, those of Keynesianism. These told us that supply was perfectly elastic, at least in the short run, and that we could forget about price responses. It was that simple way of looking at the economy that encouraged generations of politicians and civil servants to believe that they could manage the economy, the level of demand and the level of unemployment.

Now we have another set of stylised facts and theories of the type proposed by Professor Minford. This approach causes erratic jumps from one policy to another. I recognise that the financial journalists have done much valiant work in the attempt to break one set of stylised facts, but I would recommend that we do not try to oversimplify the issues. We should admit that the world is complicated. Although I much prefer the set of stylised facts offered by Professor Minford to those of the Keynesian school, we must realise that they are open to the charge of over-simplification and that, on these grounds, its opponents may reject the theory completely.

I should like to make a point on currency convertibility that Professor Rose omitted to mention, namely that the abolition of exchange control entails two kinds of response. The first we might term the 'bureaucratic response', where the order to control M3 suddenly makes life very complicated, and the bureaucrats have to scratch around to try to find ways to patch up the new holes in the control system.

The other type of response is the recognition that currency convertibility in its own right and in its own way exercises considerable control over both the government and the banks, and far less attention needs to be paid to any bureaucratic response. With luck the problem of sterling fades away. We may even reach the kind of wonderful picture that Professor Minford has painted, in which the rate of inflation might well be one million per cent, but no-one would care since no-one would be using that currency. The correct response to the abolition of exchange controls is to say that it is a splendid occurrence since it makes us shift our attention away from artificial methods of controlling inflation.

TIM CONGDON: My question relates specifically to the monetary base proposal. The trouble with it is that, over a very long period and in virtually all countries, central banks have not operated on the monetary base. Advocates of the proposal need to explain why this is so. I think there is a very good reason. What matters in all economies is the money supply—by which I mean cash and bank deposits. Let us forget about the M3, M2, M4 muddle and think solely in terms of cash and deposits. We regard deposits as being on a par with cash because we can always convert them into cash. Now that belief is basic to financial confidence. It is part of the notion that the banking system is sound, reliable, trustworthy and so on. Central banks found from experience that they had to be willing to supply the system with cash when it wanted it. The purpose was to ensure that the banking system was sound.

That is the underlying reason why no system of monetary base control has been applied anywhere for long. There have been very brief examples: for instance, in Britain between 1844 and 1847 when the Bank Charter Act, which embodied the monetary base idea, was in force for three years and then had to be suspended. I will not go into the ramifications of that, but Professor Rose did say that the banking system had operated in its present form only since 1914. That is not correct. Before 1914 the Bank of England always provided cash to the banks when and in the quantities they wanted it. Bagehot put forward the golden rule that, whenever the banking system wanted cash, the central bank must provide it and achieve control by the rate of interest charged on its loans.

Professor Rose's suggestion concentrated on bankers' balances at the Bank of England and not notes and coin.

ROSE: That was simply to prevent the issue becoming too complicated.

CONGDON: The difficulty there is that it presumably has to remain a characteristic of the system that bankers' balances are convertible into cash. So if there is no control over cash there is no control over bankers' balances either.

In practice, a bankers' balance arrangement is virtually what exists at present. We do have a $1\frac{1}{2}$ per cent bankers' balance requirement on the clearing banks. They have to abide by that; not exactly every day, but it is their target. There is no fundamental change in going over to a bankers' balance system with a higher ratio, say 6 or 7 per cent. The real issue is whether the banks are going to be refused assistance at some point.

Finally, insofar as the bankers' balance requirement differs from what the banks would want for their own business reasons, it is a distortion. At the moment, for example, the clearing banks complain that $1\frac{1}{2}$ per cent is too high and they would be happy with something like $\frac{3}{4}$ to 1 per cent for their clearing activity. In both America and Germany, where a bankers' balance (or reserve requirement) system obtains at present, the banks dislike it and try to get round it. In America they leave the Federal Reserve system or push the money offshore. The same is also happening, to some extent, in Germany through the development of an offshore market.

What I am getting at is that it has to be explained why the system of readily available central bank cash accommodation developed, why it is almost universal, and why it has lasted for so long. I suspect advocates of the monetary base have not thought hard enough about these questions.

SELDON: It seems clear that we have two views here. Personally, I am always more sceptical about the powers and intentions of government than are some of my friends (like, for example, Milton Friedman), who seem to me, in some respects, macro-statists. They think that, once government knows what it has to do in monetary policy, it will—and can—do it. In that respect, I remain much closer to Hayek in doubting both propositions: government is not necessarily able to do it; nor, even if it is capable, does it want to do it. We must be concerned with incentives and motives as well as with technical aims and methods.

ROSE: I think that we are all of one mind that if there is to be a monetary policy at all, it has to be compatible with a commercial banking system. That is very different from saying that the Bank of England is necessarily right in arguing the need to provide liquidity for the system on a day-to-day basis.

The technical problem of monetary policy, however, is less important than the question of fiscal policy. Nonetheless, I cannot accept Michael Beenstock's argument, if only because in practice monetary targets have been crucial to the problem of keeping fiscal policy under control. I find it difficult to believe that, if there were no monetary policy target at all, the general financial policies that are required would be achieved. If this is the case, there has to be a choice from the whole spectrum of possible financial targets of one which is going to be effective without causing too much damage.

Danger of 'fine-tuning'

To go from Keynesian fine-tuning to monetarist fine-tuning would simply be to compound the fundamental philosophical weaknesses of past policy, and I would agree entirely that far too much time is spent worrying about the short-run behaviour of M1 or M3 or M5. One of the reasons is that the technique of policy places so much emphasis on the long-term bond market, where the gains and losses from being right or wrong are very considerable indeed. Part of the problem is that monetary policy operates in an administrative sort of way, with large jumps in MLR and so forth. So much time is spent in poring over the entrails because of the need of financial operators to take a view on these large steps. The sort of monetary policy I would want is one in which rates of interest were left more to themselves and where large jumps in MLR rarely took place; where it was taken for granted that rates were going to fluctuate and it could be left to private risk-takers to decide whether it was worthwhile to act as stabilisers.

If that sort of policy and the present sort are both rejected, what form of policy is there to be? Do the authorities fix the level of interest rates? I cannot believe that that is the right sort of policy if only because of the classic statement that it is real rather than nominal interest rates that matter, and nobody knows what the real interest rates are. If Michael Beenstock is arguing that we need somehow to control a wide spectrum of financial assets, it would be a return to the bottomless pit of 'liquidity' into which the country nearly sank.

So while I agree entirely that, compared with other issues, the monetary base question is comparatively minor, it is not one that we can ignore, if only because it does have an effect on these other and more important issues.

3. The Need to Cut Public Expenditure and Taxation

WALTER ELTIS

Exeter College, Oxford

The Author

WALTER ELTIS: Fellow of Exeter College and Lecturer in Economics, University of Oxford, since 1963. He was Visiting Reader in Economics at the University of Western Australia, 1970, Visiting Professor of Economics, University of Toronto, 1976-77, and at the European University Institute, Florence, in March-April 1979. He has been a general editor of *Oxford Economic Papers* since 1974 and he was an Economic Consultant to the National Economic Development Office from 1963 until 1966. Since 1977 he has been Economic and Financial Consultant to Rowe and Pitman. He is the author of *Growth and Distribution* (1973); co-author with Robert Bacon of *Britain's Economic Problem: Too Few Producers* (1976); and he has published articles on Adam Smith and François Quesnay. For the IEA he contributed 'How Growth in Public Expenditure has Contributed to Britain's Difficulties' (with Robert Bacon), in *The Dilemmas of Government Expenditure* (Readings 15, 1976), and 'Public Policy', in *Job Creation—or Destruction?* (Readings 20, 1979).

Arthur Seldon: *As a taxpayer, I am all ears to hear how my taxes will be cut. Walter Eltis has circulated a new sheet with an even more enticing title in which he is going to tell us how taxes can be cut more than public spending.*

I. HIGH OR LOW PUBLIC EXPENDITURE/TAX RATIOS?

It is now widely agreed that the need to control the money supply sets a limit to the public sector borrowing requirement (PSBR). That borrowing requirement can be achieved with high or with low ratios of public expenditure and taxation to the National Income. What are the advantages in having low rather than high ratios of public expenditure and taxation, when in both cases the borrowing requirement is the same?

The Keynesian high spending/high taxing solution

The conventional Keynesian answer to this question is that high public expenditure and tax ratios will produce a higher National Product than low ones because of the balanced-budget multiplier theorem. If public expenditure and taxation are both raised by £1,000, the government will definitely spend its £1,000, but the extra taxation will not cause the private sector to spend a full £1,000 less. It will pay part of the £1,000 tax increase by cutting its rate of saving. Hence total demand will be raised by an equal increase in public expenditure and taxation,[1] and this will also raise supply if the economy is at all below full employment.

Hence the Keynesian position is that, with higher public expenditure and taxation, demand, employment and presumably also company profitability will generally be higher. Those of the trade

---

[1] Including the full multiplier effects, the extra government spending of £1,000 will raise demand by £1,000 $(1+c+c^2+c^3+c^4 \ldots)$, where c is the marginal propensity to consume home-produced goods and services, while the £1,000 of extra taxation which is needed to sustain a balanced budget will cut demand by only £1,000 $(c+c^2+c^3+c^4 \ldots)$. Hence an increase in both public expenditure and taxation by £1,000 will raise effective demand by £1,000, so the balanced budget multiplier is 1.

union leaders who have economics degrees will have learned this analysis, because it was universally taught in British universities until quite recently. The balanced-budget multiplier analysis is also programmed into all the Keynesian computer models of the economy. The moment any government speaks of cutting both public expenditure and taxation, such computers will predict that the National Product will fall, because the lower expenditure will *all* be taken out of effective demand, while only *a fraction* of the lower taxation will be added to demand.

The alternative: cutting spending and taxation *can* raise output

In face of this line of argument, how can it possibly be maintained that cutting public expenditure and taxation will raise the National Product? No British O- or A-level examiner would have contemplated the possibility that the opposite of the balanced-budget multiplier proposition might be true, say, 15 years ago, but there are four lines of argument that suggest that output and employment will become *higher* at low public expenditure and tax ratios than at high ones.

(i) *Incentive to work*

First, a low public expenditure and tax ratio makes it possible to increase the economic incentive to take work for those on low incomes. If lower-paid workers pay less taxation when they have jobs, but receive the same social security benefits when they are unemployed, which is practical when aggregate public expenditure is lower, they are more likely to accept jobs—and they will find them more quickly. The 'natural' rate of unemployment will then become lower, and if unemployment approximates to the natural rate over the cycle as a whole, the average level of output will be higher if average unemployment is lower.

(ii) *Lower cost of labour*

Secondly, lower public expenditure and taxation makes it possible substantially to reduce the cost of employing labour. This should raise employment and output in the market sector of the economy because employers will offer to employ more workers if the cost of employing them is lower.

(iii) *Reduced capital/labour conflict*

Thirdly, with *falling* public expenditure and tax ratios, the sum of total wages and profits in the market sector of the economy will rise faster than with stable public expenditure and tax ratios, because the government will take a diminishing slice from the extra incomes that result from higher output. This should reduce the degree of conflict between capital and labour. Co-operation is often the solution to positive-sum games, while conflict is inevitable in zero- and negative-sum games.

(iv) *Incentives to entrepreneurship*

Finally, there are the well-known incentive effects to entrepreneurship which should result from lower taxation.

Lowering the natural rate of unemployment

The first line of argument on the 'natural' rate of unemployment is entirely straightforward. It is widely agreed that in Britain the unemployment rate at which the labour market balances has risen by something like one million or by about 4 per cent of the total labour force since the early 1960s. Table I shows how 'domestically-generated inflation' decelerated between 1964 and 1967 when

TABLE I

UNEMPLOYMENT AND INFLATION: GREAT BRITAIN, 1964-80

	Unemployment	Domestically-generated Inflation	Natural rate of Unemployment
	%	%	%
1964-67	1·5—1·8	4·0, 3·9, 2·8	Less than 1·5
1967-71	2·4—2·6	2·8, 3·2, 3·7, 7·8, 10·6	More than 2·6
1971-73	3·5—3·8	10·6, 10·1, 7·6	Less than 3·5
1973-75	2·6—2·7	7·6, 17·2, 27·2	More than 2·7
1975-78	4·2—6·1	27·2, 14·2, 11·2, 10·6	Less than 6·1
1978-80	5·5—6·0	10·6, 12·0, 15·0	More than 5·5

Note: Domestically-generated inflation is approximated by the GDP deflator at factor cost. This leaves out of account inflation due in the first instance to higher indirect taxation and higher import prices, which are both largely independent of the domestic labour markets with which the natural rate hypothesis is concerned.

unemployment was between $1\frac{1}{2}$ and 2 per cent. It took an unemployment rate of between 4 and 6 per cent to produce decelerating inflation from 1975 to 1978, and inflation accelerated in 1978-80 with an unemployment rate of over 5·5 per cent.

The labour market is said to be in equilibrium with a *stable* rate of inflation when unemployment is at the 'natural' rate. It used to be possible to achieve a stable inflation rate with $1\frac{1}{2}$ to 2 per cent unemployment, but it now seems only possible to achieve stable inflation with more than $5\frac{1}{2}$ per cent unemployment. Hence the unemployment rate at which the inflation rate does not take off and get faster, year after year, appears to have risen by a million or so. In the early 1970s Mr Edward Heath had to put unemployment up to almost one million to stop the trend of accelerating inflation. Mr James Callaghan had to increase it to well over a million to break the trend of accelerating inflation. Mrs Margaret Thatcher took over an economy in which inflation threatened to get faster year by year at an unemployment rate of around a million and a half.

Vacancies and 'voluntary' unemployment

The vacancies figures tell a similar story. Many consider vacancies the real test of the tightness or otherwise of the labour market, a high vacancies figure indicating a particular degree of shortage of labour. In the second and third quarters of 1978, when there were 210,000 vacancies, there were 1,377,000 unemployed. In the first quarter of 1973, when there were 218,000 vacancies, there were 751,000 unemployed. In the second and third quarters of 1969, when there were 212,000 vacancies, there were 535,000 unemployed. In the first half of 1964, when there were 207,000 vacancies, there were only 435,000 unemployed. Thus a similar number of vacancies is now associated with 900,000 more unemployed than it used to be. This is also the case at higher and lower vacancy figures than 210,000 to 220,000.

It should be unnecessary to add that, despite almost $1\frac{1}{2}$ million unemployed in 1980, London Transport, British Rail and the Post Office cannot get enough workers to run these essential services without unacceptable delays to passengers and to letters. There are thus considerable areas of labour scarcity at an official unemployment rate of 6 per cent or more. This is explicable if there is a large element of voluntary unemployment in the labour market.

Ratio of unemployment benefits to average earnings

The rising ratio of unemployment benefits to average earnings net of tax is obviously a factor in the explanation of this state of affairs. According to recent data by Spindler and Maki,[2] social benefits for a family with two children averaged 40·7 per cent of net-of-tax earnings in 1961, 45·7 per cent in 1965, 54·1 per cent in 1966, 69·7 per cent in 1967, 73·1 per cent in 1968, 76·6 per cent in 1972, after which they fell back to 69·5 per cent in 1975. The sharp rise from 1961 to 1972 coincides with part of the rise in the natural rate of unemployment, but the further increase between 1972 and 1980 is not readily explicable by a further increase in the ratio of unemployment benefits to earnings. The measurement of unemployment benefits and earnings is of course complex and controversial, but it would be widely agreed that the unemployment-benefit-to-earnings ratio is a factor of some significance. Spindler and Maki believe that its increase may explain $\frac{1}{2}$ to 1 per cent of the 4 per cent increase in the natural rate of unemployment, which still leaves most of it to be explained by other factors.

This conclusion may understate the influence of a high ratio of unemployment benefits to earnings, for this factor will allow workers to be costlessly militant, since the lost jobs which result from militancy may cost many workers little in cash. Such effects on union militancy are bound to act slowly through union power and the attitudes of those who elect union leaders and shop stewards. If they have little to lose from militancy, militants will be elected, and that will then raise the natural rate of unemployment after a time-lag. But that is only speculation. The hard evidence points to only a modest inter-connection between the unemployment-benefit-to-earnings ratio and the natural rate of unemployment.

If a government can get its aggregate expenditure down so that lower-paid workers face less taxation while unemployment benefits are unchanged (on the assumption that their amount is determined by a society's assessment of social 'need'), the ratio of earnings to benefits will rise. The natural rate of unemployment should then become slightly lower—one can only say 'slightly' from the hard evidence—and average output over the cycle slightly higher in

---

[2] Z. A. Spindler and Dennis Maki, 'More on the effects of unemployment compensation on the rate of unemployment in Great Britain', *Oxford Economic Papers*, March 1979.

consequence. That is one inter-connection between the public expenditure and tax ratio and the level of output which goes the opposite way to the Keynesian relationship. It will be a strong force in the opposite direction to Keynesian orthodoxy only if it can be shown that there is a strong link between the unemployment-benefits-to-earnings ratio and the natural rate of unemployment.

It may be added that, even if there is a strong link, a lower natural rate of unemployment will only be translated into lower unemployment in the long run when unemployment really is at the natural rate. In the short term, unemployment may be far higher than the natural rate, so that lower public expenditure and taxation increase the willingness to take jobs when extra jobs are not in practice available. That is, however, only a theoretical possibility. In practice there are vacancies which some of the lower-paid will not take, and any changes in taxation which make those jobs acceptable will lead to an immediate rise in employment and output.

II. INCIDENCE OF TAX CUTS: EFFECTS ON LABOUR COSTS AND OUTPUT

There is a second principal way in which an economy's aggregate ability *to supply* will be higher where taxation is lower.[3] When taxes are cut, some of the benefit will go to labour in the form of higher wages net of tax, and some to capital in the form of higher profits net of tax. There are many ways in which various taxes can be passed forwards or backwards between capital and labour, so it is best to focus attention only on where they ultimately fall. If the total taxes levied per worker employed are 50 per cent of the total cost of employing a worker, this cost will fall by $\frac{1}{2}$ per cent if taxes are cut by 1 per cent and the whole benefit goes to the employer. If only half the benefit goes to the employer, a 1 per cent reduction in rates of taxation will result in a $\frac{1}{4}$ per cent reduction in the total cost of labour. If labour costs $\frac{1}{4}$ per cent less, more workers can be expected to be employed.

---

[3] The line of argument that follows owes much to a seminar which Professor W. M. Corden gave in Melbourne in July 1979. His argument will be published in the *Economic Journal* in 1981.

In general, if taxation forms T per cent of total costs, and a fraction q of the benefits of tax cuts go to cut the cost of employing labour, while (1-q) goes to the worker as a higher net-of-tax income, a 1 per cent tax cut will cut the cost of employing labour by q.T per cent. In the above example, q is one-half and T is 50 per cent so q.T$=\frac{1}{4}$, and therefore a 1 per cent tax cut reduces the cost of employing a worker by $\frac{1}{4}$ per cent, but the formula has general validity. There will always be some reduction in the cost of labour after a reduction in taxation provided part of the benefit goes to the employer. With all the uncertainties of incidence theory it would be astounding if the entire benefit from tax cuts always went to the worker and none to the company that employed him—especially when we remember that some of the taxes that are now levied are employers' national insurance contributions where lower rates of tax ought very clearly to cut the cost of employing labour.

How tax cuts which reduce labour costs raise employment

How will a cut in the real cost of labour influence employment and output? Imagine an economy where value-added per worker with the most efficient plant and in the most efficient firms is 50 per cent higher than that in the firms which are barely on the margin of profitability. In such an economy, a 50 per cent increase in the real cost of labour would make all firms unprofitable. Those that were formerly barely profitable would have to pay wages which exceeded the value of their output by 50 per cent, while even the most profitable firm in the economy would be pushed to the point where it could only just cover its wage bill with nothing to spare. Soon afterwards, all the firms in the economy would close down because none could cover their wages with a bare margin for profit. Hence if value-added per worker in the most efficient part of the economy exceeds that in the least efficient activities by 50 per cent, a 50 per cent real wage increase would wipe out all employment in the private market sector. If wages rose 10 per cent, it would be a reasonable approximation that this would cut employment by $\frac{10}{50}$; if wages rose 1 per cent, this could be expected to cut employment by $\frac{1}{50}$.

More generally, if value-added per worker was X per cent higher in the most efficient firms and plants than in the least, a 1 per cent rise in real wages would cut employment by the fraction $\frac{1}{X}$. This is because an X per cent rise in wages would destroy all employment, so a 1 per cent rise in wages would simply destroy a fraction, $\frac{1}{X}$, of total employment. A 1 per cent cut in the real cost of labour could, with similar reasoning, raise market sector employment by $\frac{1}{X}$.

The various strands of the argument can now be brought together. If tax amounts in total to a fraction, T, of the cost of employing labour, and a fraction, q, of tax cuts goes to companies (while workers receive the remainder (1-q)), a 1 per cent cut in taxation will cut the cost of employing labour by q.T per cent. This will then raise total employment by $\frac{q.T}{X}$ per cent. Thus if T is 50 per cent, X is 50 per cent and q is one-half, a 1 per cent cut in taxation will raise employment by $\frac{1}{2}$ per cent. In Britain T averages out at about 40 per cent, while X may be something like 80 per cent.[4] Hence, if the benefits from tax cuts are shared equally by workers and companies, so that $q = \frac{1}{2}$, $\frac{q.T}{X}$ will equal $\frac{1}{4}$, so a 1 per cent cut in taxation will raise employment by something like $\frac{1}{4}$ per cent. This is, of course, a very crude approximation, but the calculation can be refined. *The vital point is that tax cuts raise employment.*

Tax rates can be cut by more than government expenditure

This proposition has an implication of fundamental importance. If tax cuts raise employment, they will subsequently raise tax revenues, because the newly-employed workers will themselves pay taxes. If tax revenue rises in proportion to employment, the following proposition emerges. Start with a public expenditure cut and a cut in tax rates of 1 per cent, and it might be thought that there would be no change in the budget deficit (or surplus). The government spends 1 per cent less, and takes 1 per cent less from each worker. But this will only leave the budget unchanged if employment is unaltered. If part of the benefit from lower taxation goes to companies with the result that employment rises $\frac{q.T}{X}$ per cent, tax revenues will fall $(1-\frac{q.T}{X})$ per cent and not 1 per cent. The cut in *the rate* of taxation will reduce tax revenues 1 per cent but the subsequent increase in employment will raise them $\frac{q.T}{X}$ per cent. That means that in all tax revenues will fall by $(1-\frac{q.T}{X})$ per cent.

---

[4] In 1978, gross profits (less stock appreciation and adjustment for financial services) were 44 per cent of 'incomes from employment'. (*National Income and Expenditure, 1979*, Table 3.1.) If they were zero in the least efficient firms and plants, they may have totalled around 80 per cent of employment incomes in the most efficient.

This reasoning produces a vital proposition. In order to cut taxes by 1 per cent, and leave the budget balance unchanged, it is necessary only to cut public expenditure by $(1-\frac{q.T}{X})$ per cent. In the example set out above, where q is $\frac{1}{2}$, T is 40 per cent and X is 80 per cent, a tax cut of 1 per cent will be compatible with an unchanged budget surplus or deficit if public expenditure is cut by $\frac{3}{4}$ per cent. That is simply an example; but the underlying principle is a general one. Because tax cuts reduce the cost of employing labour, and hence raise employment *and the tax base of the economy,* tax rates can safely be cut by more than public expenditure. In the above example, tax rates can be cut by 1 per cent for each $\frac{3}{4}$ per cent cut in public expenditure. The public expenditure cut finances a $\frac{3}{4}$ per cent tax cut, and the remaining $\frac{1}{4}$ per cent is financed by the larger tax base which results from the lower cost of employing labour.

The converse of this line of argument is also crucial. A tax *increase* of 1 per cent will finance a public expenditure increase of only $\frac{3}{4}$ per cent. It is an error to think that an increase in tax rates of 1 per cent will allow public expenditure to rise 1 per cent, because the 1 per cent rise in taxation raises the cost of employing labour and therefore reduces the tax base. Hence, $\frac{1}{4}$ per cent of the 1 per cent rise in tax rates is lost as a result of the reduced tax base and it is financially sound to raise public expenditure only $\frac{3}{4}$ per cent. If it is raised a full 1 per cent (and a Keynesian would consider himself utterly prudent to raise expenditure as much as tax rates), there will be subsequent disappointment because of the negative effect of the higher cost of labour on the tax base. Tax revenues would rise by only $\frac{3}{4}$ per cent because of this. Hence, while the initial intentions were prudent, the end-result would be that public expenditure would rise by a full 1 per cent and tax revenues by only $\frac{3}{4}$ per cent with the result that one-quarter of the extra public expenditure would need to be financed by borrowing.

Truly prudent public finance therefore requires that rates of taxation be raised by more than public expenditure. Conversely, they can safely be cut by more than public expenditure, and the proposition is that a $(1-\frac{q.T}{X})$ public expenditure cut suffices to finance a 1 per cent tax cut.

That, then, is the second line of argument in favour of lower public expenditure and taxation: that it enlarges employment and the economy's total tax base. This argument, and the previous one about the effect of lower taxation on the cost of 'search', and therefore on the equilibrium level of voluntary unemployment, are in the mainstream of neo-classical economic analysis. It is quite straightforward to argue that an increase in the net-of-tax incomes of the employed relative to the unemployed will reduce voluntary unemployment. It is equally straightforward to argue that more employment will be offered at the lower cost of labour that will result from lower rates of taxation. Lower rates of taxation will therefore increase both the employment that is offered and the employment that is taken according to the most straightforward economic analysis. There is therefore no difficulty in proposing these two reasons why an economy will produce more where taxation and public expenditure are lower. The only difficulty is in quantifying the benefits.

III. IS OUTPUT DEMAND- OR SUPPLY-CONSTRAINED?

A Keynesian might argue that the balanced-budget multiplier is superior because, in the real world, output is demand- and not supply-constrained. Higher taxation and public expenditure do nothing for supply but they do plenty for demand. In contrast, the neo-classical effects which have been put forward in favour of lower public expenditure are both supply effects. They do nothing for demand. So is British long-term output supply- or demand-constrained? If it is demand that is lacking, and not supply potential, the Keynesians and their former pupils, the trade union leaders, may be right after all.

So how can one argue that it is the supply constraints that really matter? One has to argue that, as a result of EEC membership, the Kennedy Round and all that, the UK economy has become a small part of the world economy. Therefore what British industry and commerce can produce and sell does not depend on British demand but on world demand for that output, and this is potentially indefinite because world demand is enormous in relation to what Britain can produce. The vital constraints are therefore supply constraints.

British labour costs, taxation and international competition

How much can British industry and commerce supply at a cost which is less at the margin than the extra sales revenue obtained?

British costs will determine how much can be supplied at a profit. If they fall, extra goods and services will become available for supply to the world and home markets and these can then be substituted for foreign goods both at home and overseas. If, on the contrary, the marginal costs of British production rise relative to the prices at which competitive products are on offer, less will be supplied, so foreign production will be substituted for British production in both home and overseas markets. British motor-cycles, for example, have to be sold at a price which competes with Japanese motor-cycles. That price determines the value-added per motor-cycle of the British industry. If the cost of labour exceeds the value-added per worker (when motor-cycles are sold at a price that competes with the Japanese), employment to produce motor-cycles in Britain cannot be offered. At a lower cost of labour, due either to a lower cost of employment per head or a higher productivity of motor-cycles and therefore a higher value-added per head, workers can be employed. Employment will therefore depend vitally in the motor-cycle industry and the others which face international competition on how much a British worker costs to employ, and on how much he is willing to produce. *These are matters which lower taxation will assist.*

The neo-classical arguments which have been outlined are at their strongest and sharpest with the assumption that Britain is a small part of the world economy where demand is always present for the products of any process of production that can provide a value-added which exceeds wage costs. The Keynesian argument that extra government-created demand in Britain raises what is supplied works most sharply if there is no foreign trade. It is the opening of so many frontiers to virtually free trade that has undermined the Keynesian argument that extra government spending raises output, and made the neo-classical tax-cutting arguments so much stronger than they used to be. Keynes and Schacht talked sense in the 1930s when British and German import propensities were far lower than today's.

IV. CONDITIONS FOR PROSPERITY AND GROWTH

There are two lines of argument in favour of lower public expenditure and taxation which do not depend so sharply on whether or not there are ample trading opportunities which allow what is produced cheaply enough to be sold. The first is based on the effect of public expenditure and taxation on the degree of industrial conflict. Table II contrasts the extra real resources available to the British and West German market sectors, where all marketed output is produced, from 1965 to 1977.

Table II shows that in West Germany there was a 91 per cent increase in real government spending on behalf of each market sector worker as against an increase of only 63 per cent in Britain. Hence the suggestion that raising public expenditure rapidly is destabilising is clearly false, for West German governments raised real government spending per worker about $1\frac{1}{2}$ times as fast as British governments. But the Germans had a 62 per cent increase in labour productivity in this period against Britain's mere 30 per cent increase. The result of Germany's 62 per cent productivity increase was that government could spend 91 per cent more on behalf of each worker and still leave

TABLE II

WHAT HAPPENED TO EXTRA PRODUCTION: BRITAIN AND WEST GERMANY, 1965 TO 1977

	1965	1977	*Increase*
BRITAIN			%
Marketed output per worker	100	130	30
Purchased by government and with government-financed incomes	35 (35%)	57 (44%)	63
Remainder available to market sector workers and companies	65	73	12
WEST GERMANY			
Marketed output per worker	100	162	62
Purchased by government and with government-financed incomes	33 (33%)	63 (39%)	91
Remainder available to market sector workers and companies	67	99	48

Source Note: The British data are derived in the manner set out in Robert Bacon and Walter Eltis, 'The Measurement of the Growth of the Non-Market Sector and its Implications', *Economic Journal*, June 1979; and the West German data are derived similarly by Dr Gerhard Willke of the European University Institute, Florence, Italy.

48 per cent extra for German workers and companies to spend themselves. In Britain productivity rose only 30 per cent, and the 63 per cent increase in government spending on behalf of each worker left a mere 12 per cent extra for workers and companies to spend themselves, that is, only 1 per cent extra each year. The German workers and companies had an extra 48 per cent over 12 years, or an extra 3·3 per cent a year to spend themselves. This meant that German workers and companies were playing a positive-sum game where both sides of industry could gain substantially. The British, with 1 per cent growth per annum for workers and companies, were in a near zero-sum game where one side of industry could gain heavily only at the expense of the other.

Growth in public expenditure in excess of productivity encourages union militancy

The result is that a co-operative British trade unionist is now in a difficult situation. If he expects the next 12 years to be like the last, he will be able to offer his members 12 per cent more over 12 years as a reward for co-operation. But what if the bargaining power of his union is such that, by disruption, 20 or 30 per cent more can be obtained? Then he will not be able to out-persuade the disrupters, who will therefore obtain control of the union membership. Union leaders will be elected who will take an extra 30 per cent where industrial action can achieve it in preference to the 12 per cent that could result from quiet acquiescence. The 20 or 30 per cent will be worth having, even if it seriously disrupts the economy, if the result of not disrupting is so mediocre. Imagine now that a militant disrupter turns up in Germany and accuses the moderate union leaders of failing to get the 30 per cent their local monopoly power may occasionally offer. The reply will be that 30 per cent is not worth having at the cost of seriously disrupting the German economy which is making 48 per cent extra available over 12 years to the average co-operative worker. The disrupters just cannot beat 48 per cent every 12 years. Hence the German workers elect moderates and the British militants, especially in industries like coal-mining where there is indeed monopoly power to exploit.

If the British government had been content to take just 30 per cent more per worker from 1965 to 1977, there would have been 30 per cent extra for workers and companies to spend, so that Britain would have been much closer to West Germany's positive-sum game where co-operation and moderation are rational. Because government took 63 per cent more *when only 30 per cent extra was produced per worker*, British companies and unions were pushed into a situation where militancy and industrial conflict were better rewarded than co-operation.

If from now onwards government spending can be held or, better still, reduced while output grows, positive-sum game conditions can be recreated in Britain. There were positive-sum game conditions in the 1950s when the government spending ratio fell and productivity grew 2 or 3 per cent per annum. Over the decade of the 1950s workers and companies gained well over 30 per cent. From 1965 to 1977 they gained only 12 per cent. If it becomes possible to offer them 30 per cent extra from 1977 to 1990 (and they have probably gained 10 per cent already from 1977 to 1980), positive-sum game conditions will begin to be restored, and the moderation of the 1950s should return.

There could be rich rewards from this movement to moderation, and above all for productivity. If productivity once starts to rise at the German rate, then government expenditure can safely be allowed to rise at the West German rate. But the key point is that productivity may only start to rise at that rate if governments leave the market sector sufficient growth in real incomes for positive-sum game conditions to prevail. This requirement means that, so long as output grows slowly, public expenditure will have to grow more slowly still, or it may even have to decline, to create the conditions where co-operation can set productivity on an upward path.

Managerial incentives

That is obviously a line of argument that statisticians will never capture, but it may still be far more important than those they can quantify. The managerial incentives arguments are also like that. Perhaps the best way to state them formally is to start with the argument where they are almost irrelevant. Some economics textbooks would state that the only considerations that interest managers are net-of-tax pay and leisure. Hence tax cuts which increase net-of-tax pay will only help the economy by causing managers to take more work (to raise pay) at the expense of leisure. But tax cuts in any case raise net-of-tax incomes so managers will perhaps take more leisure even though they could earn still more by giving up a day of leisure. Because of the lower taxation, they can have more money and more leisure to spend it in, so why should they work more? Perhaps they will, but it is not clear why they should.

Tax cuts and risk-taking

Suppose, in contrast, managers are interested in money net of tax, leisure, and, in addition, security and quiet, comfortable and conflict-free working conditions. They can then substitute extra money for less leisure, or less security or a less quiet and comfortable life while at work. That opens up many more ways in which tax cuts can make the economy more efficient. Managers can be expected to take more risks. Where marginal taxation is 83 per cent, a successful venture involving new technology and products may have virtually no effect on net-of-tax incomes. An unsuccessful venture, on the other hand, can destroy a reputation. So the odds are heavily weighted against risk-taking. What is the use of extra money at 83 per cent taxation when set against a lost reputation if things go wrong? At 60 per cent taxation, in contrast, there will be quite a lot of extra money. The risk may now be worth taking. Here income is being substituted for security.

Take another example where under the old tax rates companies could not pay executives as much money as they wished to. So management substituted perks and quiet working conditions, lavish office facilities, no sacking for the inefficient, and acquiescence in union inefficiencies (to save ulcers). Now that it is possible to offer higher monetary rewards, there should be less tolerance of the inefficient money-substitutes that managers were so often fobbed-off with in place of high incomes for the more successful.

The effect of lower taxation on managerial efficiency could be the strongest effect of all, but it is not a measurable effect, so its importance will never be proved.

Questions and Discussion

PATRICK MINFORD: It is not necessary to be above the natural rate of unemployment for your second (Laffer) argument to work. So, presumably, the other side of the equation of increased demand for labour is an increased supply of labour due to its elasticity of supply by employees. That is fully consistent with unemployment being continuously at the natural rate.

WALTER ELTIS: The supply of labour, I thought, was in my first line of argument about the influence of the rate of taxation on the natural rate of unemployment.

MINFORD: I interpreted that as an argument about the amount of equilibrium search activity; this is an argument about the supply of effort. The first relates to the stock of unemployed workers, the second to a flow.

ELTIS: I see. It helps the drift of the argument.

JOHN BURTON: I would have thought that there were arguments for cutting government expenditure other than the four mentioned. One would be the Keynesian 'crowding-out' argument, which Keynes put forward himself. It argues that a high level of government spending is itself, perhaps, deleterious to investment intentions in the private sector. There are other arguments—legions of them— which can be dragged in to justify lower government spending and taxation, not just the four.

JOHN WOOD: For the record, it is assumed, is it not, that other factors determine the natural rate of unemployment in addition to the relationship between social benefits and earnings—trade unions, housing, geographical mobility, and so on?

ELTIS: Yes, obviously, but the cost of search is the one which costs money. Legislation on industrial relations should certainly help to bring the natural rate of unemployment down, but this will not cost government money so it is independent of the rate of taxation and public expenditure. Union legislation by the 1974-79 Labour governments made it easier for militants to win strikes in the past few years, and this may have contributed to the rise in the natural rate of unemployment by raising the critical unemployment rate at which the rate of inflation accelerates.

MORRIS PERLMAN: I am not sure that it will reduce the cost of search. Cutting taxes does increase the cost of search because the current income lost from searching rises. But, if taxes are cut, future income rises by the same amount because the real wage that is found from searching is also changed by the tax-rate change. If rational decisions are taken in terms of costs—marginal costs in standard equations—I am not sure that the net benefit from searching will change when both the cost of search and the gains from search are changed in the same proportions.

ELTIS: Three numbers have to be borne in mind: what a man gets when unemployed; what he would get in the job that he could take easily; and what he would get in the better job he could find only with difficulty. Altering the tax rate changes the ratio of the first to both the second and the third, so there can be a variety of possible effects.

What is in my mind when I use the word 'search' is that many unemployed people are not actively searching for work, because they prefer leisure. 'Search' is simply a more comfortable way of describing voluntary unemployment. If the key trade-off is indeed between leisure and net-of-tax income from work, there should be a clear-cut benefit from raising the income from work relative to unemployment benefits.

WILLIAM REES-MOGG: To take the argument back to a point discussed earlier, there comes a choice. If cuts in government expenditure could be achieved there would come a choice of whether to use those cuts to reduce taxation or to reduce the PSBR. In circumstances like the present, can we not rationally expect that the benefits of a lower PSBR, even in terms of the prospects for output and employment, are likely to be greater than the benefits of a cut in taxation?

ELTIS: That is a very good question, and it would indeed merit a session to itself. The level of interest rates at present must be a severe deterrent to economic activity of all kinds, and one would expect this to be closely associated with the very high level of the PSBR. The argument in my paper separated out this effect by asking whether a given level of the PSBR should be achieved with low public expenditure and taxation in preference to high public expenditure and taxation. To ask whether there should be a low PSBR or low taxation is a different question altogether. To attempt to answer it: the first task for Britain now is to squeeze inflationary expectations out of the economy. No pleasant economic developments can be expected until that is done, and it will take a couple of years or more. So, until late 1981 or 1982, growth may be irrelevant, thus favouring the immediate case for cutting the PSBR rather than taxation—which is, in effect, what the Government is doing.

ARTHUR SELDON: I am rather foxed. Government apologists will claim that the Government has cut taxes; yet its critics, such as Denis Healey, say there has been no increase in output. My conclusion would be not that tax cuts are not right, but that they are not large enough. Nigel Lawson, for example, would argue that this Government has cut taxes on incentive pay. And so my question would be: How far do taxes have to go in order to yield a large enough increase in tax revenue to enable taxes to be cut more than public outlays and so avoid higher borrowing? What extent of tax cuts do you have to achieve in order to boost effort and output and enterprise and so on in order to get a large enough increase in the tax base and, therefore, a large enough increase in revenue, to avoid more borrowing if you are cutting taxes more than expenditure?

ELTIS: There is no doubt that cutting the top rate of income tax to 60 per cent is a large change which should influence managerial incentives. So far as the cost of employing labour is concerned, it would be quite extraordinary if Mr Lawson was briefed to say that this Government had reduced taxation. When both indirect and direct taxes are taken into account at a constant real income level, I would be astonished to find there had been any cut at all for the average worker.

SELDON: The Government's argument is that the cut in direct taxes has a more stimulating effect on incentive and effort than the increase in VAT has in reducing effort by raising prices.

ELTIS: That is a different argument. The total cost of labour depends on both direct and indirect taxation.

SELDON: But I thought it was official government policy to alter the structure of the disincentives. How far, therefore, do cuts in taxes on income and investment, and so on, have to go before you get a large enough boost in production and therefore in tax revenue? I do not see much evidence of it yet.

ELTIS: There is no evidence because there has been no cut in *overall* taxation. I would use the word 'tinkering' to describe the substitution of indirect for direct taxation while leaving the total tax burden on labour unchanged. The safe argument to use is that, if the total tax burden, direct and indirect, is cut, workers do have something to pass back to the employer. If, on the other hand, the overall burden stays the same, reliance has to be placed on the second-order effects such that the tax which is raised is a little less damaging than the tax which is reduced. The Government has not been able to cut the cost of employing labour because it has not been able to cut public expenditure in real terms; and the beginning and end of it so far as the ordinary worker is concerned is that there have been no tax cuts to pass back. There may indeed be a little extra taxation for workers to try to pass on to their employers.

SELDON: Then what we are left with is higher borrowing?

ELTIS: Yes, or higher taxation.

SELDON: I do not like that: neither is desirable.

ELTIS: No, indeed not. But my paper has argued the case for cutting public expenditure, so that the worker is given something that he may actually partly pass back to the benefit of his company.

HAROLD ROSE: To what extent does the general argument turn on marginal rates of taxes as opposed to average rates of taxes?

ELTIS: The formula in my paper has a constant and proportional rate of tax of T per cent, so T is both the average and the marginal rate of tax. If the marginal rate is altered in relation to the average, the details of the argument will obviously be affected, but not its overall nature.

ROSE: The other question is: If tax cuts are linked, what importance should be given to cutting the taxes of those people paying tax or to raising the threshold?

WOOD: The primary purpose of this gathering is not to think in terms of immediate or practical policies, but it does help to have them at the back of one's mind. I am now a little confused by Walter Eltis's agreement with William Rees-Mogg that the most beneficial effects on output would follow from taking the benefit of lower expenditure on the reduced PSBR *via* the interest rate effect, rather than the alternative, which was *via* the incentive effect through unemployment. Which does Mr Eltis prefer?

ELTIS: My paper was concerned with the case for lower public expenditure and taxation *at a given borrowing requirement*. I did not also discuss the case for a lower borrowing requirement. But if I was asked to say how I would deal with both questions at the same time I would say: get public expenditure down. This gives the scope for future tax cuts. But, initially, until inflationary expectations are squeezed out, the borrowing requirement should be reduced, not taxation. Then, when a resumption of growth is possible, tax cuts should be implemented to reinforce the growth rate. In other words, my staging would be: get the monetary side right first—possibly with some attention to the cost of search at the beginning since a higher cost of search could make the period when the economy is flat more comfortable as there should be less strike action.

MICHAEL BEENSTOCK: As one who has tried to estimate this aggregate Laffer curve for the UK (the result seeming to point to the overall effect that, if the average burden of taxation in the community is cut, there is a favourable supply response),[1] I would still like to express a few words of caution. First, the theory does not really say which way the incentive effect will go; that is an empirical issue. I would say that there is a net incentive effect. But many people would disagree. And, in the way the discussion has been presented, it seems to have been taken for granted that there will be a favourable effect, even though economic theory is agnostic on this point. Consequently, I would not lay great policy emphasis here because I would rather lay it on those things which have strong *a priori* justification in economic theory—rather than on something which theory says could go either way. Here I would agree with William Rees-Mogg that the PSBR is more important than taxation.

Secondly, great care is needed in discussing public expenditure, certainly in the aggregate. It makes a lot of difference to the supply side of the economy whether the government cuts back on, say, academic salaries, or whether it cuts back on things that do matter to the running of the economy, such as roads. Reductions in public expenditure can, through micro-economic effects, jeopardise the supply side of the economy.

ELTIS: Michael Beenstock is doing an injustice to economic theory. This is obviously a large subject, but what produces his result that the effect of lower taxation on supply could go either way is that it has both an income and a substitution effect on the ordinary worker which influences the amount of effort he puts in. With *higher net-of-*

---

[1] M. Beenstock, 'Taxation and Incentives in the UK', *Lloyds Bank Review,* October 1979.

tax incomes he may need to work less; but with a bigger marginal net-of-tax reward from an extra hour's work he may *substitute* work for leisure. The overall effect could obviously go either way if that is all there is to it. But my argument about the effect of taxation on the *cost* of employing labour does not rest on effort. It rests on the cost of labour. Economic theory has plenty to say on the subject of how the cost of labour influences employment, and it is not at all difficult for economists to argue that the benefits from tax cuts go partly to workers and partly to the companies that employ them. So Michael Beenstock is not taking into account the argument that the cost of employment is a factor that influences employment and output. I agree that there is an ambiguity about the supply-of-effort argument which I accepted very happily from Patrick Minford.

ROSE: Unless you postulate some exogenous real income aspiration, the assumption that a cut in tax is passed on must really turn on the substitution effect, must it not?

ANTHONY COURAKIS: All that is needed is to assume that the supply of labour is not downward-sloping, which is what I understood Michael Beenstock to be saying. It is not necessary to assume that it is horizontal, but merely that it is not downward-sloping. If it is downward-sloping, then Mr Eltis's case, as I understand it, is the extreme one in which the taxed income of the wage-earner is allowed to remain the same while an incentive to the firm is retained.

ELTIS: No, I am saying only that the benefits from tax cuts are shared in some way.

COURAKIS: But even if they are shared, would not the effect be the same?

ELTIS: It would be extraordinary if tax cuts went entirely to wages, or entirely to profits. They must surely benefit both.

MINFORD: The point is that, with Keynesian unemployment, and thus wage rigidity, there is an infinitely elastic supply of labour. So it would all be passed back, and the effect Walter Eltis describes would be substantial through the demand side. But I am uncomfortable with this because, typically, it is assumed that the economy adjusts to some natural rate; the very use of the term 'natural rate' implies it. Then the issue of supply elasticities arises. I would support Mr Eltis there; the bulk of theory and evidence—a great deal of it in the case of developing countries where backward-bending supply curves were once thought to be very likely—suggests that there are positive supply elasticities of labour.

BEENSTOCK: I would say that the main empirical research initiative in this country on incentives and labour supply, financed by the SSRC, has concluded the opposite.[2]

MINFORD: That is just one drop in a very large empirical ocean. Work in this country is, in any case, rather limited.

ELTIS: Three comments in conclusion. First, I would be astounded if, with a reduction in, for instance, employers' national insurance contributions, there was no favourable effect on the cost of labour. So the sole argument I need is: cut the employers' social security contributions, thus cutting the cost of employing labour, which should then have an effect on employment in accordance with well-known neo-classical arguments. I would reiterate that, if the cost of employing labour is reduced by cutting social security contributions, there will be a neo-classical effect on employment which can go only in one direction.

Secondly, the economic theory which appears in many textbooks is simplified by having managerial utility (U) depend solely on leisure (L) and net-of-tax financial rewards (W(1-T)). That is:

$$U=f(L, W(1-T)).$$

With a simple utility function like this, cutting T can be beneficial only by persuading managers to take less leisure (L) and more income (W), and this effect could be weak or non-existent. But by introducing security of income (S), placidity at work (P) (that is, no conflict with unions about traditional work practices), then:

$$U=f(L, W(1-T), S, P).$$

Higher net-of-tax income can be substituted for job security (S) (that is, managers can take more risks), and it can also be substituted for perks, on-the-job leisure, and a placid attitude to inefficiency (P). Thus the scope for favourable effects from lower taxation is substantially widened.

---

[2] For example, A. B. Atkinson, N. H. Stern and J. Gomulka, 'On Labour Supply and Commodity Demands', in A. Deaton (ed.), *Essays in the Theory and Measurement of Consumer Behaviour*, Cambridge University Press, 1980.

Finally, there is the argument which follows from Laffer's well-known diagram. A superficial civil servant might predict that an increase in tax rates towards 100 per cent would produce a situation where tax revenues rose towards 100 per cent of national income, so that tax yields followed the line AB in my diagram. The well-known insight for which Laffer is celebrated is that the curve does not go from A to B where, at a 100 per cent rate of tax, government gets the whole national income. He reminded us that at a 100 per cent rate of tax there would not be any taxpayers—because either they would be somewhere else or they would have arranged, legally

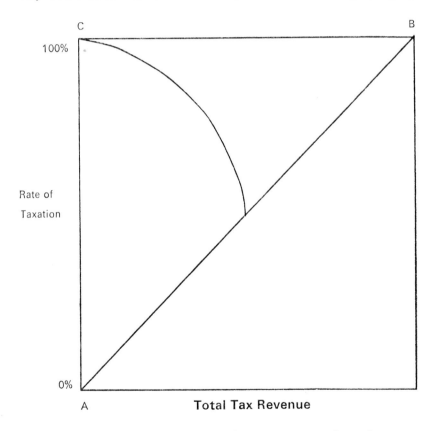

or illegally, not to pay tax. At a 100 per cent rate of tax the curve would be at C and not B; hence there must be some tax rate below 100 per cent where the curve turns leftwards towards C instead of continuing to B. This piece of economic theory is far older than Laffer, but Sir Robert Peel and people like him did not draw the curve. The curve makes it clear without a shadow of doubt that you must get some favourable supply effects as you reduce taxation from 100 per cent downwards to a certain point. On that I rest my case.

4. Charging for Non-Public Goods?

MORRIS PERLMAN

London School of Economics

The Author

MORRIS PERLMAN was born in Cracow, Poland, in 1937. He received a BBA from the City University of New York in 1961, and a Ph.D. from the University of Chicago in 1966. He was Assistant Professor of Economics at Cornell University in 1965-66, joined the London School of Economics as Lecturer in Economics in 1966, and is now Senior Lecturer.

His publications include 'Forced Savings and the Rate of Interest' (*Journal of Political Economy,* March/April 1971); 'The Rôles of Money in an Economy and the Optimum Quantity of Money' (*Economica,* August 1971); and *Macroeconomics* (Weidenfeld and Nicolson, London, 1974). For the IEA he contributed a British commentary to Gordon Tullock's *The Vote Motive* (Hobart Paperback No. 9, 1976).

I. CHARGING FOR GOVERNMENT SERVICES AND THE PSBR

When I considered the title of this Seminar, 'Is Monetarism Enough?', I asked, probably as did many others: 'Enough for what?' I assumed the answer to be: 'Enough for solving some of the macro-economic problems facing Britain: inflation, unemployment and the low rate of growth of output'. When I was asked to talk about charging for government services, it was not clear to me how my topic was connected to the issues raised by the title of this Seminar. After reading some of the papers and listening to the discussions I assume that the connecting link in some people's minds is the Public Sector Borrowing Requirement (PSBR), and the emphasis placed on controlling it. Thus charging for government services will provide revenue which can be used to reduce or to control the PSBR more effectively, and this may result in more effective control of the money supply or of interest rates.

Now, though I am a monetarist and believe that the money supply should be controlled, I am a Chicago monetarist of the old school. I believe that the money supply can be controlled whatever happens to the PSBR and, moreover, that the size of the PSBR tells us very little about the government's contribution or otherwise to the solution of the macro-economic problems facing Britain.

Danger of the artificial creation of 'joint goods' in ideas

I emphasise these points because I am wary of the artificial creation of joint goods (where in order to purchase one good you must purchase another with it). Such joint goods phenomena in the market are explained as an attempt by a monopolist to make his monopoly power more effective. Package goods in ideas have a similar explanation; namely, if one believes that an idea is true or 'saleable', it can be conjoined with another idea in an attempt to sell the package. That is inefficient and dangerous. If one of the ideas turns out to be wrong—and all our ideas might turn out to be wrong—both ideas are likely to be thrown out at the same time.

II. EFFICIENCY AND DISTRIBUTION

I shall therefore discuss the question of charging or not charging from the point of view of the two micro issues it raises—those of efficiency and distribution. Both issues have been well explored.

Public goods and efficiency

In standard economic theory there are some goods, called 'public goods', which should be provided by government since they cannot be provided efficiently by the private sector, either because they cannot be charged for, or because for various reasons it is inefficient to do so. On the same grounds of efficiency, however, the production and consumption of other goods should be decided by individuals. Of all the expenditures on goods and services undertaken by government in Britain, very few would come under the 'public goods' heading of standard economic theory. Police, defence, lighthouses— that traditional text-book example—are public goods, and perhaps one can include the fire services. But these constitute a very small proportion of expenditures. The major part of public expenditure is on social services: health services, education, personal social services, housing, and other, smaller, services such as refuse collection. So on grounds of efficiency, and with traditional theory and the traditional concept of what we mean by a 'public good', there is very little justification for any of these services to be provided by government. If they were to be provided centrally at all, presumably one would argue for charging for them, on standard economic efficiency grounds. There is one point I want to make about that.

Difficulty of defining 'public good'

The specification of what is a public good is itself problematic. Public goods like defence must be provided by government and financed through taxation because of the 'free-rider' problem: if the government provides defence, I am defended whether I contribute to its provision or not, and I cannot be excluded from its benefits. However, the framework of this kind of theory is also one which allows that the nature of a public good is in some sense determined by what society thinks is a public good. Is education a public or a private good? In terms of the ability to exclude it is of course a private good since I can stop somebody coming in to a classroom, and can teach only those in the classroom. But if it is argued that the good provided by education is not simply sitting in a classroom but, perhaps, a more intelligent electorate which will give us a better democratic system, then this benefit becomes a public good in terms of general economic theory.

I do not want to argue that the concept of public goods is not useful, but that, like most other concepts, it must be used with care.

Inefficiency in mobility

Up to now I have been dealing with the standard efficiency argument for charging for goods which are not public. Another kind of efficiency argument for charging is important in Britain where many of the goods are provided by local government rather than by central government, even though they are highly subsidised. Around 60 to 65 per cent of local authority expenditures is paid by grants, i.e., from the general tax system, but the provision is made by local decision. Different authorities provide different kinds of goods or different qualities of goods. There, is therefore, another possible efficiency problem of providing goods 'free', i.e., not charging a price equal to a relevant concept of cost, namely, inefficiency in mobility. This is known as the Tiebout effect.[1] People will base their location decisions partly on the provision at zero cost of particular goods. This raises another set of efficiency issues for the question of charging for local authority services.

The other reason given for governmental provision of goods at zero cost to the individual consumer, financed through the tax system and borrowing, is to achieve distributional goals. The argument against zero-cost provision of services to achieve those distributional goals is that even if one accepts the goals, there might be a more efficient way of achieving redistribution—whatever degree of redistribution one wants. This may be done through a tax system, a voucher system, or some other system which will achieve the distributional goal yet avoid the inefficiencies implied in redistribution by supplying particular commodities.

---

[1] The net cost of living in a particular area is the difference between the local taxes paid and specific benefits less charges in that area. (Charles M. Tiebout, 'A Pure Theory of Local Public Expenditures', *Journal of Political Economy*, 64, October 1956, pp. 416-24.)

Redistribution of income—negative income tax

If one is worried solely about income distribution, the most efficient way of changing the income distribution is by redistributing income itself and allowing people to spend it in whatever way they wish. This could be done through the tax system using, for example, a negative income tax, and then deciding on the provision of services, and their pricing on efficiency criteria. We would thus achieve both efficient provision of services and efficient redistribution.

This argument is particularly strong in a system where the provision of goods is by local authorities. Redistribution varies across local authorities. If I live in an area in which there is a lot of redistribution towards me *via* the provision of services, the net redistribution (net of rates) may be different for me than for somebody else living in a different area, though our incomes are the same. The argument for achieving redistribution by a negative income tax is that it should be effected by the central government, rather than through a multiplicity of local authorities. Then and only then are equal people ('equal' defined as equal in terms of income, or whatever the criterion for redistribution is), treated equally.

The reaction against achieving distributional goals through a negative income tax has been strong both here and in the United States. One reason is that it would reduce the power and the income of the multiplicity of agencies currently concerned with income distribution. But I do not believe that is the only reason. One reason for wanting redistribution of income is because one is worried about the income of others; one has some moral or ethical reason for not allowing anybody's income to fall below a certain level.

But there is also a more paternalistic reason. Roughly defined, paternalism here would mean not only that government is worried about somebody's income, although that might be part of it, but also that they are concerned about his expenditures, about the choices he might make, and they therefore wish to distribute income to him so he can (and will) consume some particular range of commodities. If, therefore, the 'poor' should have health and education of particular sorts, they cannot be given income to allow them to purchase these commodities unaided, because they may spend it on 'bad things', whatever these may be, and the paternalistic goal of redistribution would not be attained. I believe this is an important barrier against achieving redistribution *via* straight distribution of income rather than *via* the provision of goods and services.

Advantages of a voucher system

However, if one is concerned both with efficiency and with redistribution, then I believe that both can be achieved, and achieved more efficiently, if the redistribution is effected through the tax system, allowing individuals to purchase the goods they desire. If there are certain elements of paternalism that should be countenanced, one can achieve these implicitly *via* a voucher system.

One can regard a voucher system as a particular kind of income limited in the range of expenditure that can be made with it. One could have a limited voucher for, say, education which must be spent on education, public or private. One could have a more general voucher which would be an amount of money to be spent on a given range of goods, say, health or education. Or one could simply give money—which is nothing more than an unrestricted voucher, i.e. the range of commodities on which it can be spent is not limited. The range over which one might want to effect this redistribution by the voucher system (from a specific voucher to acquire a specific commodity, possibly even from a specific supplier, to the most general voucher which is money) depends on what underlies the goals of distribution.

These are briefly the kinds of arguments and issues involved in charging for services and governmental provision of services—the micro issues. Nothing above, no arguments and no element in these arguments, is based on the effects of these decisions on the rate of inflation or employment. They are arguments concerned solely with efficiency and distribution.

III. CHARGING IS NOT A MACRO-ECONOMIC QUESTION

Let me return briefly to my opening remarks. To reduce government's involvement in the provision of certain goods, or to increase the charges for the goods provided by local authorities *because* this would lead to a more efficient and viable economic system, is a valid argument. However, to increase charges because this would raise government revenue and allow a reduction in the PSBR is not. Such an argument would never persuade me, nor would I advocate it.

I believe that the money supply can be controlled without worrying about the PSBR. A method of doing so was discussed when Professor Rose talked about the cash reserve system. Of course, even with such control, changes in the PSBR and in the types of assets provided by government will affect interest rates. Large fluctuations in the PSBR with control of the money supply will lead to fluctuations in interest rates. If these are considered undesirable that may be a reason for financing the 'correct' amount of government expenditures with taxes rather than borrowing. But the allocation of expenditures between the government and the private sectors, and the issue of charging, must be made on other grounds.

I think that on grounds of both efficient resource allocation and efficient redistribution there are sufficiently powerful arguments for changing the types of services provided by the government, and the structure of charges, without resort to the second order effects of such changes on the PSBR.

Questions and Discussion

ARTHUR SELDON: Speaking as one who is not unbiased on this issue, I should like to say that there is one other aspect that Dr Perlman seems to have omitted from his talk: if the reduction of government expenditure is the objective—and some of us seem to think that it is a long-term, not a short-term, aim—macro methods, like cash limits or expenditure ceilings, are not an efficient way of reducing expenditure on non-public goods. There is a case, therefore, for introducing more pricing, not because it has no defects of its own (it has) but because the macro measures that the government has used almost exclusively for the control of expenditure on non-public goods, and which take up a larger part of government outlay than Dr Perlman has allowed, are so inefficient that there is a case for seeing how far micro controls might be introduced.

PATRICK MINFORD: I agree with that. If public spending has to be cut, the obvious way is through charging rather than through cutting essentially private goods that people want; this is the main connection between the topics.

MORRIS PERLMAN: If government spending has to be cut, the decision to charge or not to charge for the provision of a public service can still be decided on other grounds. If public spending has to be cut, then cut it. Even though I am sympathetic—I would be quite willing to slice a very large fraction off all government expenditure —I would not use these arguments to justify it. The allocation of expenditure between the private and public sectors has to be argued on grounds that have nothing to do with monetarism, which is a theory of the effects of certain types of financing on inflation and other macro-economic variables.

MINFORD: But the two things are linked because of the correct wish not to raise taxation on the one hand, essentially on micro grounds, combined with the macro wish—which Dr Perlman does not agree with, but let us take it as given—to cut the PSBR. It just so happens that the two alternatives are either to charge or to cut spending on goods or services. Cutting spending on goods or services would, ironically, make the micro distortions worse because it would cut things that people would want in a system in which there was market determination of demand for them. For example, the way in which cuts get implemented in the present situation is that local councillors concentrate them on the areas of maximum political sensitivity, perhaps partly in order to slow them down. Consequently, expenditure is being reduced in the least appropriate areas and not in the areas where micro-economic considerations suggest it ought to occur. So there is not only an analytical link; it happens that at this moment there is also a close practical link.

RUSSELL LEWIS: If the cutting is left in the hands of the civil servants, they cut services. The objective of the civil service is eventually to cut out services altogether, leaving only the civil servants. That is the logical extension of their behaviour.

ALAN BUDD: There is no real disagreement here. I would like both to cut the public sector deficit and to increase charges in the public sector. Even if I did not want to cut the deficit, I might still want to increase charges in the public sector. So the two are compatible.

PERLMAN: Yes, they are compatible but one is not the reason for the other. On grounds of both efficiency and redistribution, I would agree with your desire to increase charges.

SELDON: Are you saying that the use of more market pricing for public and other goods will have almost no useful macro effects?

PERLMAN: It will have efficiency effects.

TIM CONGDON: It may be that we can regard these topics as distinct and separate. I believe in cutting the PSBR and in extending the range of the price mechanism, without regarding the two things as parts of one argument. But it is intriguing that the kind of people who believe in sound money and cutting the PSBR are also the kind of people who believe in charging for public services. There may be a convincing logic behind this. Goods provided by the market have to be paid for with money. Moreover, private agents face uncertainty and have to keep money about them as a precaution. On the other hand, in the public sector, allocation decisions, decisions about planning services, and so on are not affected by liquidity. Bureaucrats do not have to worry about that side of things at all. That may be a reason why supporters of sound money are also in favour of extending the price mechanism into what is, at present, the public sector. Even if the beliefs are distinct, there may be a good explanation for the overlap in the sort of people who hold them.

ANTHONY COURAKIS: That is a bit too subtle. With regard both to controlling the money supply and to paying for services, the position taken by Morris Perlman is a rather old one. Although I am not sure about the details, because it is quite some time since I read *Capitalism and Freedom*, there is a lot in common with Milton Friedman on that particular point. While the same instincts motivate control and steady growth of the money supply, there is no reason why in any particular circumstance the PSBR, the control of the money supply, and so on, ought to be considered a necessary prerequisite for deciding on the free-market provision of some services and the chance to provide them in the public sector or *vice-versa*. We need not go on to any convoluted arguments; it is just an attitude towards minimum government interference, and that is all.

CONGDON: That is fine. I was not suggesting that one argument was a justification for the other. I was just saying that the same kind of people tend to advance both arguments. There may be a logic to that, reflecting a particular underlying philosophical disposition. There is another link: where rapid inflation is taking place, markets do not work well and there is a tendency to favour the political rather than the private provision of services.

SELDON: Is it not true that, if the emphasis government puts on macro controls could be reduced and applied to a smaller range of its expenditure, its job would be easier? And the more its job was eased, the more it could use other controls on other parts of public outlay through pricing. The more that a government used market prices as a discipline on its own expenditure on some goods, the more it would to some extent facilitate its own job of using macro-economic controls, like cash limits or expenditure ceilings, since it would be reducing the expenditure over which it would have to reinforce them. In that sense is it not right that an increased use of micro pricing, or charging for those goods which lend themselves to discipline on expenditure by pricing, would ease the job of the Treasury in devising and applying macro-economic rules?

HAROLD ROSE: But we must surely not fall into the trap of wanting the public suppliers of these services to act as monopolists charging monopoly prices to enable them to finance the rest of the public sector. We must appear to say that the rest of the public sector can be more easily financed.

SELDON: Higher charges would, of themselves, reduce the size of the unnecessarily large public sector by switching demand. If there was to be charging for library books, for example, it might be found that W. H. Smith and Boots suddenly restored their book-lending business.

LEWIS: It is not true to say that those who believe in a limited money supply are necessarily supporters of the free market. The Soviet Union believes in restricting the money supply, but does not seem to have much time for the free market. The crucial link between a limited supply of money and the free market is the idea that people ought to pay the true price of things.

SELDON: Government is going to have to ask the local authorities to control some of their outlays by increases in charges, and it will have to empower them to raise prices for some goods where they already have the power to charge, and contemplate extending the range of chargeable services. Government is going to find it easier to control the Rate Support Grant by reducing the extent to which it has subsidised local government up till now.

5. Trade Unions' Role in the British Disease: 'An Interest in Inflation'?

JOHN BURTON

University of Birmingham

The Author

JOHN BURTON is a Lecturer in Industrial Economics, Dept. of Industrial Economic and Business Studies, University of Birmingham. Previously Principal Lecturer in Economics at Kingston Polytechnic. He has been an economic consultant to the National Board for Prices and Incomes, the Office of Manpower Economics, and the OECD. He is the author of *Wage Inflation* (1972), and of articles in the journals. He contributed a paper, 'Are Trade Unions a Public Good/'Bad'?: The Economics of the Closed Shop', to IEA Readings No. 17, *Trade Unions: Public Goods or Public 'Bads'?* (1978); joint author (with J. M. Buchanan and Richard Wagner) of *The Consequences of Mr Keynes* (Hobart Paper 78, IEA, 1978).

Arthur Seldon: *Now to a topic which once caused a certain amount of division among the hierarchy of the IEA, almost to the point of splitting the atom. There are two views on this subject. Some of us share the view of Milton Friedman that the trade unions play no independent or direct 'cost-push' part in the causation of inflation. This is a fairly extreme statement of his view; a more refined version is that the old-fashioned importunity of government may* indirectly *induce it to enlarge M1, M2, M3 or M4, and thus to inflate in a direct 'demand-pull' fashion.*

I. INTRODUCTION

I would like to make some introductory observations that struck Morris Perlman as well as myself. The general title of this Seminar is 'Is Monetarism Enough?' and the first point that needs to be made is that it begs the question of what 'brand' of monetarism we are being asked to consider. There is a wide variety of schools of monetarist analysis. We have discussed some of them this morning. There is rational expectations monetarism, Friedmanite monetarism, then again there is the international quantity theory, and also fiscal monetarism.[1]

I appreciate the difficulty that Hamish McRae was talking about in trying to get this point—that 'monetarism' is not a monolithic paradigm—over to people. But I do think that it is a very important political point that *must* be got over. We hear politicians such as Mr Healey and Mr Heath voicing their misgivings about monetarism, but they never define which sort of monetarism they are talking about. And it is important because there are considerable differences between the policy implications of the various types of monetarist analysis.

The other question begged by the title of the Seminar is: Is monetarism enough for *what*? Clearly, monetarism of whatever variety is not 'enough' if you have goals of public policy *other* than

---

[1] For a survey of the varieties of monetarist analysis, see J. T. Addison and J. Burton, *The Explanation of Inflation: Monetarist or Socio-Political Analysis?*, Macmillan, London (forthcoming).

that of containing inflation. No monetarist claims that controlling money supply is a panacea for the cure of *all* economic maladies. It is a school of thought which is mainly concerned with the containment of inflation as a policy objective, and not with the other features of what might be called 'the British economic disease'.

Symptoms of the British disease

There is some dispute about the nature and origins of the British disease, but it is the containment of the British disease *as a whole* which is—or should be—the basic objective of economic policy. There are three symptoms of the disease: high inflation, high unemployment, and low growth (and low levels) of efficiency. Monetarism is not enough to deal with that three-headed monster, for two reasons.

First, as I said earlier, it deals only with one aspect of the disease —and that is inflation. It cannot deal with the other two aspects of the disease; nor does it pretend to.

Secondly, monetarism in and of itself is concerned only with what we might call the proximate determinants of inflation. Essentially, all that monetarists claim is that the *proximate* cause of inflation is the rate of growth of the money supply in excess of the growth of real output. But the question lying behind that is: What causes money to grow fast?[2] It may well be that trade unions, for example, are not the direct 'furnace' of inflation—they may be a thermometer of inflation (as Friedman puts it) in this sense—but they could also be the 'bellows' heating the furnace of inflationary monetary growth.

I would like to draw on an analogy here that Friedman has himself used—the analogy between inflation and drug addiction. He points out that once you get used to monetary addiction of the economy, it is rather difficult to kick the habit and there are withdrawal symptoms. But this is only *one* aspect of the problem of reducing inflation. A further, more fundamental, problem is that if you give heroin addicts what is called the 'cold turkey' treatment— if you try to cure their addiction by cutting off their supply of drugs —you often find that they go back to using the drug (in probably 80 per cent of cases) after they have gone 'cold turkey'. And the

---

[2] The distinction between the proximate and fundamental causes of inflation is discussed at more length in J. T. Addison, J. Burton and T. Torrance, 'On the Causation of Inflation', *Manchester School,* Vol. 48, 1980 (forthcoming).

reason is that the *fundamental* causes of their disease—the reason why they were taking the drug in the first place—have not been cured. Unless you cure that, they are likely to go back to heroin after they have gone through the withdrawal period. As with addiction to heroin, so with addiction to inflation: the problem goes deeper; the fundamental causes of the disease have to be treated.

II. THE ROLE OF THE UNIONS IN THE BRITISH DISEASE

I will now briefly spell out the rôle of trade unionism in three aspects of the British disease, as I see it. Part of the analysis will, of necessity, be speculative; but I think it is a necessary background if we are to talk about the proper policy responses.

(i) Trade unions and inflation

First, what about trade unions and inflation? To summarise, the sheer weight of the evidence, so far as I can see (appertaining to a large number of countries and periods), suggests that neither trade unions nor any other set of private institutions are the proximate source of inflation.[3] The question really is whether they are a fundamental cause of inflation in the sense that they are the 'bellows' heating the monetary growth furnace, as I mentioned earlier.[4] I think there is some evidence, and some reason, to suggest that they may well be an important factor in inflation in this manner. A study by Willett and Laney[5] on the causes of monetary growth in Britain and Italy found that wage inflation, as well as the budget deficit, may be an important determinant of monetary growth in the two countries. Other studies have come to a variety of conclusions, but there is some empirical evidence that trade union pressure may be a cause of monetary growth here.

---

[3] J. Burton, *Trade Unions and Inflation*, Macmillan, London (forthcoming).

[4] The spectrum of economists' views on this matter is discussed in J. Burton, 'Unionism, Inflation, and Unemployment', *Vie et Sciences Economique*, July 1980.

[5] T. D. Willett and L. O. Laney, 'Monetarism, Budget Deficits and Wage Push Inflation: The Cases of Italy and the U.K.', *Banca Nazionale del Lavoro Quarterly Review*, No. 127, December 1978, pp. 315-331.

A question that intrigues me is: Why is that? Why have trade unions got a demand, as it were, for inflation? What are they getting out of it? I think that what is happening is that the possibilities of redistribution in the private sector of the economy through union action are rather small. Firstly, profits are not some vast bottomless purse which trade unions can dip into. As Professor Phelps Brown has pointed out,[6] if the whole of dividends and interest paid out by British companies in 1971 had been sequestrated and applied to raise pay (without *any* provision for those who had lost retirement incomes or trust and insurance funds), average earnings would have been raised by less than 14 per cent—and that would have been *once and for all.* So the 'bottomless purse' of profits is very small indeed.

Secondly, the other source of getting higher incomes, in the private sector, for any union is, of course, non-union employees. An estimate by the late Harry G. Johnson and P. Mieskowski suggested[7]—I quote their own words—

'that most if not all of the gains of union labour [in the United States] are made at the expense of non-unionised workers and not at the expense of earnings on capital.'

I am going to argue that even these gains from non-union labour —as with all monopolistic gains—are subject to strong forces of erosion. First, the monopoly rents of trade unionists become eroded, in the long run, by the escalation of the pecuniary price (such as entrance fees), or by the escalation of the time price (e.g. lengthy apprenticeships) that have to be paid to gain entry to the union. Second, the successful attainment of monopoly rents, as Professor Gordon Tullock has pointed out,[8] encourages other groups to monopolise and to play the same 'ball game'. Thus, in the long run, the possibilities of capturing income from non-unionised workers start to decline.

---

[6] E. H. Phelps Brown, 'New Wine in Old Bottles: Reflections on the Changed Working of Collective Bargaining', *British Journal of Industrial Relations,* Vol. XI, No. 3, 1973, p. 334.

[7] H. G. Johnson and P. Mieskowski, 'The Effects of Unionization on the Distribution of Income: A General Equilibrium Approach', *Quarterly Journal of Economics,* Vol. LXXXIV, No. 4, November 1970, p. 560.

[8] G. Tullock, 'The Welfare Costs of Tariffs, Monopolies, and Theft', *Western Economic Journal,* June 1967, pp. 224-232.

Union gains from the public sector

That leaves one major source of redistribution towards unions—redistribution through the public sector. That is, it is possible for certain groups to exploit what may be called 'fiscal illusion', since people find it difficult to comprehend the true costs of the vast array of government services for which they are paying *via* taxation. That element of fiscal illusion is considerably enlarged once there is a Keynesian fiscal constitution, which allows the use of 'hidden' forms of taxation (such as taxing future generations or the inflation tax).[9] It seems to me that the interest of unions in, and their rôle in generating, inflation lies in this attempt to exploit fiscal illusion and thus to redistribute income to themselves. This possibility arises from their indirect and direct political power: that is, their 'power' in the ballot box, and their direct lobbying power.

At the same time, of course, taxpayers in general also constitute an implicit lobby, and the outcome of the tension between the unions' political demand for subsidisation and nationalisation (which is effectively a demand for subsidisation), and the taxpayer's resistance to extra taxation, means that governments have recourse to the inflation tax and debt issuance to try to get out of these forces which are crowding in upon them. It is thus possible that trade unions do play a rôle in inflation by inspiring monetary growth, and by making the PSBR larger than it would be in the absence of their political actions. They would seem to be doing it because they gain from inflation—or rather from the public expenditures that the inflation tax finances.

(ii) Trade unions' effect on unemployment

I now turn to the question of the effect of trade unions on unemployment—the second aspect of the British disease I have itemised. Economic theory suggests that an increase in union monopoly power would not *necessarily* raise the natural rate of unemployment in the long term. It might do so *temporarily*, but a combination of competition and flexible wages in the non-union sector, and a growth of union power in the unionised sector, would simply lead (in the long run) to the displaced workers from the union sector moving into the non-union sector where wages would be (relatively) depressed,

---

[9] J. M. Buchanan, J. Burton, and R. E. Wagner, *The Consequences of Mr Keynes*, Hobart Paper 78, Institute of Economic Affairs, London, 1978.

so that total employment would eventually get back to its original level. If, however, there are other features preventing relative wage falls or wage adjustments in the non-union sector, then a growth in union power could lead to a higher natural rate of unemployment—if there are 'floors' on the level to which wages can fall in the non-union sector.

There do in fact appear to be such 'wage floors' embedded in the British economy:

(a) The Wages Councils set legally enforceable minimum wages in various trades, which covered about 3 million workers in 1970.

(b) The Central Arbitration Committee has the power to force wage (and other) conditions on non-union employers that are specified by a trade union, even though it is not recognised as a bargaining agent by the employer.

(c) There is also, of course, the unemployment/social security payments provisions. It appears to be the case, from the evidence, that not many people who become unemployed have a ratio of income out of work greater than 100 per cent of their income from work. Typically it is lower than that.[10] However, the wage in the non-union sector cannot fall below the level of the income obtainable out of work *plus* the premium necessary to induce people to work at all. These two combined set a floor on wages in the non-union sector.

So I would suggest that there are a variety of factors which, with the growth of union power over the last decade (how significant quantitatively I do not know), have probably been factors in raising the natural rate of unemployment in the UK.

(iii) Trade unions' effect on efficiency and growth

Thirdly, there is the question of the effect of unions on efficiency and growth. I would suggest that the 'static' effects of trade union power on efficiency—in terms of both allocative efficiency and X-inefficiency—are probably quite small. The allocative or output loss suggested by an American study is less than one-tenth of 1 per

---

[10] A. B. Atkinson and J. S. Flemming, 'Unemployment, Social Security, and Incentives', *Midland Bank Review*, Autumn 1978, pp. 6-16.

cent.[11] Another more recent study, for Canada, gets it up to two-tenths of 1 percentage point of national income.[12] I have suggested that in Britain it could be up to 3 per cent of national income, because we have a much higher degree of unionisation, and higher union relative wage effects too.[13]

I think, however, that the real question about the effect of trade unions on efficiency is that of their effect on long-term growth prospects and the process of economic evolution. Here I believe that we should not simply 'blame' the unions, but the whole vast variety of lobbies that exist in Britain—sectional interest groups that prevent economic adjustments taking place in declining firms and industries and, in so doing, also inhibit the growth of newcomers to the economy. This idea, that trade unions and other lobbies/sectional interests undermine long-term growth processes, is called the 'Olson hypothesis'.[14] Samuel Brittan has given his support to it.[15] The hypothesis does tie in with quite a wide body of evidence on growth data.

III. PROPOSALS FOR DE-FUSING UNION OBSTRUCTIONISM

What are the possibilities of de-fusing that trade union element in the three aspects of the British disease I have discussed? I will run through a number of proposed strategies that have been put forward over the last few years.

---

[11] A. Rees, 'The Effects of Unions on Resource Allocation', *Journal of Law and Economics,* Vol. 6, October 1963, pp. 69-78.

[12] S. Christensen and D. Maki, *Unions and the Public Interest: Essays on Collective Bargaining and the Social Costs of Union Power,* Fraser Institute, Vancouver, 1979.

[13] J. Burton, 'Are Trade Unions a Public Good/Bad? The Economics of the Closed Shop', in L. Robbins, *et al., Trade Unions: Public Goods or Public 'Bads'?,* IEA Readings 17, Institute of Economic Affairs, London, 1980, pp. 31-52.

[14] M. Olson, *The Political Economy of Comparative Growth Rates,* University of Maryland, Department of Economics, November/December 1978 (mimeo).

[15] S. Brittan, 'How British Is the British Sickness?', *Journal of Law and Economics,* Vol. XXI, No. 2, October 1978, pp. 245-268.

'Buying-out strategies'

First, there are what may be called the 'buying-out strategies'. One possibility for buying-out trade union obstructions has been put forward by Mr Brittan,[16] who suggests that government should give people in the key public sector industries job property rights in return for their giving up the strike-threat. Another, suggested by Mrs Thatcher before the 1979 General Election, would be that government should give a real-income guarantee in return for zero strikes in those key public industries. The general argument for a buying-out approach is, of course, that you are likely to reduce union resistance to change if you give a pay-off to union members.

There is, however, a basic problem with all variants of buying-out, as has been pointed out by Professor Charles Rowley, that it is rather like trying to buy out an extortionist.[17] Trade unions are engaged in the economics of extortion—demanding payment for not harming others, or 'demanding money with menaces'. The difference between trade unions and protection rackets is that the unions have been given the legal right to practise extortion, whereas the Mafia have not (although the Mafia have realised this—that if they can colonise a few unions they will have a *licit* means of running protection rackets against businesses, under the cloak of unionism; that is what they have managed to do in the United States[18]). Buying out an extortionist requires that you turn to your friendly local leg-breaker and say: 'If I give you a lump-sum payment instead of my weekly protection sub., will you go away forever more?' The problem with that approach is that he is likely to go round the corner, stuff it in his pocket, come back the next day and say: 'That's fine—now we'll have the next payment as usual!' That is why Charles Rowley calls a buying-out of union obstructions the 'Danegeld solution': you cannot buy off extortionists so easily.

I will admit there is certainly a serious problem confronting the buying-out approach here, but I would be a little bit more sanguine

---

[16] S. Brittan, 'The Political Economy of British Union Monopoly', *Three Banks Review,* September 1976.

[17] C. Rowley, 'Buying Out the Obstructors?', in S. C. Littlechild *et al., The Taming of Government,* Readings 21, Institute of Economic Affairs, London, 1979, pp. 107-118.

[18] R. Boehm, *Organized Crime and Organized Labor,* Foundation for the Advancement of the Public Trust, Arlington, Virginia, 1976.

than Rowley. It may be possible to build into a buying-out contract some means that would prevent the union from returning for more Danegeld. Suppose, for example, that in industries where strike activity had been 'bought out', trade unions only had a conditional immunity from the law of tort, so that if they broke their no-strike agreement civil actions could be brought by the injured parties. Thus it might be possible, with certain changes in the law, to enforce buying-out deals with unions. Therefore I would not entirely jettison the buying-out approach.

Conversely, we can say that buying out would appear to require changes in the law to be effective. Simply giving racketeers or unions a lump sum, and hoping that they will desist from further threats, would not work.

Worker ownership a negative solution

Another major strategy for removing union obstructions to economic reform has been suggested by Peter Jay. This is a variant of the buying-out approach. Mr Jay suggests in his Wincott lecture[19] that we buy out trade unions by offering workers ownership—the entire property rights in the enterprises in which they work.

This idea is really an entirely 'negative' case for worker ownership. Jay is not suggesting that worker ownership is efficient; he is arguing that it is the *only* possible way out of the British disease, which he diagnoses as completely and utterly terminal. Jay claims that worker ownership would de-fuse the three aspects of the British disease by confronting workers with all the entrepreneurial realities that confront their present employers. They would thus learn to set their own rates of pay in the market context. This would remove union push on wages, and thus the need to accommodate it by monetary means. Workers would get the gains from industrial improvements in their own concerns, so the barriers to inefficiency would be dismantled.

I am going to argue that Jay's preferred solution would do nothing to cure the trade union aspects of the British disease. Indeed, it would probably make them worse, for the following reasons.

A substitution in the property rights system in the form that he proposes would not do away with the basic problem of confrontation

---

[19] P. Jay, *Employment, Inflation, and Politics,* Occasional Paper 46, Institute of Economic Affairs, 1976.

between different collective interests in the labour market.[20] First, there would still be conflict within enterprises between different groups of workers. A good example of this is what happens in British universities and polytechnics, which are a sort of externally-financed form of workers' co-operative. As every academic knows, much time is spent in squabbling with other departments over the allocation of resources. Amongst groups of workers less noted for their industrial docility than academics, these potential conflicts between groups within the firm over differentials or resources could well break out into wildcat strikes and counter-strikes—as happens in Yugoslavia.[21]

Secondly, there would still be conflicts between groups of worker co-operatives. Indeed, it is likely that trade unions, instead of 'withering away', as Jay presumes they would under worker owner-ship, would re-constitute themselves as the organising arm of indus-trial cartels of worker co-operatives. If anything, as Mr Brittan has noted,[22] we could see a worsening of free collective chaos as a result of worker ownership. Such a system would lower the costs of trying to exploit other groups; instead of having to go on strike they would simply have to hike up prices across the industry and clobber them that way.

A third problem with worker ownership is highlighted by what has happened in Yugoslavia. One of the forces that undermine the possibility of enterprise monopoly in capitalism is the continuous invention of new products, and the emergence of new firms. Yugoslavia has experienced for many years a declining number of enterprises, and a very low birth rate of new firms. The basic reason is that any firm set up by an individual would eventually be trans-formed into a worker co-operative—and the individual's ownership rights removed. So the inflow of new enterprises, and the under-mining of enterprise monopoly they bring about, would be much reduced under a worker ownership régime.

---

[20] J. Burton, 'The Political Economy of Free Collective Chaos', *Focus,* Issue 1, 1980, pp. 1-11.

[21] L. Sirc, 'Workers' Management under Public and Private Ownership', in B. Chiplin, J. Coyne, and L. Sirc, *Can Workers Manage?*, Hobart Paper 77, Institute of Economic Affairs, 1977, pp. 49-86.

[22] S. Brittan, 'The Political Economy of British Union Monopoly', *op. cit.*

Unions' legal immunities cause of 'free collective chaos'

Worker ownership is not a solution to the free collective chaos of contemporary industrial relations. You cannot get away from the problem: if you want to de-fuse the clash of rival group interests that is going on now between labour cartels that have got legal immunities to threaten or harm other groups, then you have got to change—to remove or greatly soften—those immunities. It is a logical requirement of dealing with the problem.

There are some other reforms that would also help. There is a strong case for enforcing a balanced-budget rule at the constitutional level, to prevent the implicit exploitation of fiscal illusion, the existence of which gives the trade unions an incentive to lobby for inflation. I would also suggest that instead of vesting property rights in workers, we vest the property rights in publicly-owned enterprises directly in the people who supposedly own them—the public. Can you imagine what would happen if people found out on 1 January each year that they were the unlimited liability owners of firms like British Leyland? Instead of getting a nice dividend from this arrangement, they would have to shell out directly to pay for the losses! People have effectively got an unlimited liability in these losing concerns at the moment: but they do not appreciate the costs imposed on them, because these costs are hidden by being financed out of general taxation. If the costs were made explicit—if they hit the public in the pocket directly—there would be much greater public pressure for the reform of the densely-unionised public enterprises. Under the scheme I have proposed, the public would have the voting power—*via* their equity ownership—to force a change in the boards (and thus their policies) of the nationalised industries.

Questions and Discussion

WILLIAM REES-MOGG: This country still suffers in a unique way from the effects of the 1906 Act which based British trade unionism on unqualified legal immunity. Almost every other country set up its trade unionism on the principle of qualified immunity. The crucial problem is the move from unqualified to qualified immunity.

A constitutional framework would have to be devised within which the trade unions could operate. As long as they remained within it, they would be eligible for immunity; if they stepped outside it, they would not. Of course, many objections can be made to this proposal; one common objection is that it would create martyrs. But, if the matter was left to civil law, so that those who had suffered damage could sue, the criminal law would be kept out and the creation of martyrs effectively avoided.

But the qualification of immunities does not seem to be the answer to all the problems. It does not, for example, answer the problem of resistance to increases in productivity by trade unions since, almost certainly, their main resistance to improvements in productivity could be brought inside whatever constitutional framework was constructed. It cannot be denied that the right to strike should be related to conditions of employment as well as to pay—and yet conditions of work (how many people are employed on the same machine and so on) are central to the problem of productivity.

On the issue of productivity, one of the most important questions is that of the structure of the trade unions. The present political climate would not allow of a serious attempt to reconstruct our trade unions in the way the German unions were reconstructed after the war. ICI reckons that the whole of the difference in productivity between their factories in Britain and Germany is accounted for by the difference in the number of unions and the number of extra men who have to be employed because of demarcations between the unions. This, too, must be regarded as a crucial question.

The only circumstance in which the government could impose on the trade unions what they should have imposed on themselves— major rationalisations and mergers designed to produce a much smaller number of industrial unions—would be a much graver economic collapse than at present. It is quite possible that a collapse will occur in due course, at which point the structures of the trade unions and their immunity will become matters for consideration.

ARTHUR SELDON: The interesting question is whether the Bridlington agreement is enforceable by market power without the aid of the law, or does it rest solely on voluntary agreement between unions?

REES-MOGG: Bridlington is, of course, an agreement between the unions—and a very damaging one, because it was like an agreement between companies that take-overs would not permitted and therefore rationalisation would be impossible. All trade union mergers have to take place by agreement and must provide adequately for the interests of the executive officers of the unions. It is on these grounds that they often fail. When, before the Bridlington agreement, Ernest Bevin was putting together the Transport and General Workers' Union, it was possible for one union to take over another by making itself more attractive to the members of the latter by convincing them that it could get them more money than their current union was achieving. That was how Bevin put the TGWU together. But, once he had done so, he did not want to expose himself to similar tactics. Thus there developed the 'hands-off' policy of Bridlington.

HAROLD ROSE: John Burton did not mention the closed shop. Is it important?

JOHN BURTON: The closed shop does raise important questions about freedom, about the freedom not to associate, but I doubt it has any considerable direct effect on efficiency. There is a case for a reform of the law to make trade unions responsible for the damages they cause to third parties, and, as a part of that, to the person forced out of employment by a closed shop agreement between a union and an employer. He ought to be able to sue both the union and the employer for the costs imposed upon him. That is but part of the general case for giving people the right to sue for damages imposed by others.

MICHAEL BEENSTOCK: A small point about damage to third parties. I can see the case for legislation. But, suppose I decide not to work—whether or not as a member of a union—so much so that someone else is affected by my decision. To have indemnification at this level would introduce a completely different concept into the British legal system. People would effectively be forced to stick to such and such work because otherwise someone else would be affected. That is very dangerous.

Let me try to tie together the macro-economic aspects we have been discussing and the micro-economics of trade unions. Obviously, the legal side is important, and the legal conventions should be extended to take in the trade unions. But to a large extent the so-called power of the trade unions has reflected the political economy of the last 25 years based on full employment, which has effectively become built-in to people's expectations. Forty years or so ago, talk of full employment policies must have sounded very strange. Once it was realised that wage shocks would not necessarily lead to unemployment because there was a government committed to full employment which seemed able, for a period at least, to achieve that end, the risks for the trade unions of making a mistake were reduced and a kind of discipline removed.

But we seem now to be moving to a different kind of political economy, and it may well happen—though it will take years to become apparent—that the so-called strength of trade unions will be reduced by the discipline of the market. There is now a wage shock in the system as a result of the concerted efforts of trade unionists to see if they can get something out of it. Monetary policy is no longer adaptive and there will be no U-turn—or so we hope—so that much of the macro-economic trade union power that has been worrying both politicians and the press will simply wither away. That will still leave the important micro issues of what to do about contract breaking and the like, but I think the macro issue is more important.

BURTON: If we can force on governments some kind of constraints on monetary accommodation, trade unions will find that they are banging their heads against a brick wall when they try to engage in wage pushfulness. But how can these constraints on government be enforced? There is a demand for monetary accommodation because people can 'play the system' and redistribute income to themselves through inflation. The real question is whether government is going to hold to its rules on monetary accommodation, or whether it will abandon them in the face of such pressures. In the absence of any *constitutional* constraints, the result will depend simply on the resolve of political leaders. They are going to find it very tough because the evidence is that trade unions affect the inflation process in another way, i.e., that the slope of the Phillips curve is flatter in the unionised sector than in the non-unionised sector. The aggregate short-run Phillips curve is flatter the higher the level of unionisation. It is likely that a move down the flat, short-run Phillips curve will have to go quite some distance and for quite some time before monetary restraint has much discernible effect on wage inflation.

ANTHONY COURAKIS: I was intrigued by John Burton's references to increases in union power over the past 10 years and by the explanation in those terms of the increase in the natural rate of unemployment. I would go along much more with Walter Eltis's explanation than with that of an increase in union power, which would in any case compare with the increase in union power in some earlier decades. Measured by whatever index one chooses (and I need hardly remind you of the quality of such indices, or of the ambiguities in their meaning), the relative increase in union power is too small to explain a movement from a range of 1·5-2 per cent unemployment and (say) 2·5 per cent 'natural rate of unemployment'[1] to the kind of natural rate of unemployment level generally inferred at present.

Further, in his discussion of the macro effects, it was not clear whether John Burton was referring to the impact of unionisation in the long or short run. For example, I was struck, in his discussion of inflation, by his view (in contrast to that of Harry Johnson and P. Mieskowski) that there are *no gains to be had from wage pushfulness*. That seemed to me to be a long-run statement.

The same applies to some of his comments about the effects of trade unions on unemployment. Again he stresses the long run, and suggests that union monopoly power has no long-run effects, except insofar as institutional constraints prevent the process of displacement from unionised to non-unionised sectors. With this exception (and institutional constraints are themselves subject to change in the long run), there is therefore a logical conclusion that unions have no effect on long-term growth since, in the long run, they do not alter relative prices.

Attention should be focussed on the effect unions have in the *short run*—that at any given point in time they reduce the mobility of labour. Insofar as they do so, they thereby raise the natural rate of unemployment as defined by Friedman, i.e. that rate 'grounded out' by the Walrasian system of relationships which, Walrasian or not, reflects the characteristics of the market, including union behaviour.

From that standpoint, also, it is perfectly clear that unions can gain; at any given point in time they will try to take advantage of any (short-run) monopoly power they exercise, since, whether it is

---

[1] This being roughly the rate that earlier estimates of the Phillips curve, which may perhaps be said to derive from an environment characterised by a zero expected rate of inflation, suggest as the rate of unemployment at which the rate of change in prices will be equal to zero and hence equal to the expected rate.

the size of the cake, the rate of growth of the money supply, the PSBR, government expenditure, or whatever, that is limited, an *individual* trade union will nevertheless attempt to increase its own slice of the cake. And in an interdependent economy the government will *properly* deem itself obliged to respond—not because it wishes to maintain employment in this union, but because it has to cause an income effect to offset the adverse substitution effect that the wage-raising union is generating, not for itself alone but also (though, of course, to varying degrees) among other groups of labour that are linked to it industrially. Here there is a much more fundamental problem arising from the *interdependence defined by present technology*.

From this standpoint the Jay proposals should be assessed in terms of their effects on *the relationship between union structure and economic interdependence*. This also bears on the issue of 'extortion' that John Burton raised. In the Jay scheme the 'extortionist' may have a different information perspective, and would certainly have a different preference function from that which the present union structure apparently reveals.

RUSSELL LEWIS: The trade unions manage to enlarge their privileges when socialist governments are in power. The closed shop —especially within a nationalised industry—means an increase in union membership; and the setting up of a body like ACAS tends to be done in such a way as to make it easier to recruit more and more worthwhile people to the union. Up to a point this is a sort of conspiracy; but some of it is accidental and just happens to coincide with socialism. Most trade unionists do not particularly want their industry to be nationalised. But, when it is nationalised, the consequences are as John Burton mentioned. Nationalisation adds another restriction to the operation of a market in employment and leads to the 'sealing off' of certain areas of industry. The important point is not that nationalised industry legislation stops wages from going down but that the peculiar set-up of a nationalised industry encourages over-manning and subsidy by the taxpayer. Thus this is a big limitation on the operation of a free labour market; employees are locked into a nationalised industry at higher rates of pay than are justified by their productivity.[2] For example, the productivity of

---

[2] This theme is discussed in some detail in Graham Hutton, *Whatever Happened to Productivity?*, Occasional Paper 56, IEA, 1980.

116

miners has fallen by 6 per cent in six years. It would not have been so bad if they had been in the private sector. The situation in the steel industry is, of course, even more dramatic.

BURTON: Union power has grown over the last decade. There has been an increase in the percentage of the workforce as a whole that is unionised from around the low forties in the early 1960s to over 50 per cent of all employees now. Furthermore, there is evidence that the relative wage effect of the unions has been rising.[3] The area of the labour market covered by the closed shop has been growing, and the changes in labour law during 1974-76 have also buttressed union economic power.[4] How important this has been, though, in interacting with other matters to produce an increase in the natural rate of unemployment is not known.

Russell Lewis raised the very interesting issue of whether this situation can be remedied so long as the trade unions finance a political party. Suppose one political party does manage to qualify their immunities. Will not the other party dismantle the legislation on its return to power? There is one possible way of avoiding this *impasse*: the attack should be directed not only to trade union immunities, but also to that other set of labour cartels—the professional associations.

SELDON: Do they have the same privileges?

BURTON: They are not trade unions in the legal sense, but they do have a lot of special privileges, occupational licences, and so on. One way of avoiding the charge that trade union reform is an anti-working class measure (although I must stress that the removal of trade union immunities would *raise* the general standard of living of the working class) would be to attack the whole spectrum of special lobbies—and especially the 'trade unions of the middle class', the professional associations. Their special privileges should also be removed.

SELDON: So we have answered the question: monetarism is not enough.

---

[3] R. Layard, D. Metcalf, and S. Nickell, 'The Effect of Collective Bargaining on Wages', London School of Economics, Centre for the Economics of Education, London, 1977 (mimeo).

[4] J. Burton, *The Trojan Horse: Union Power in British Politics,* Adam Smith Institute, London, 1979.

IEA READINGS in Print

1. Education—A Framework for Choice
Papers on historical, economic and administrative aspects of choice in education and its finance
A. C. F. Beales, Mark Blaug, E. G. West, Sir Douglas Veale, *with an Appraisal by* Dr Rhodes Boyson
1967   Second Edition 1970 (xvi+100pp., 90p)

2. Growth through Industry
A re-consideration of principles and practice before and after the National Plan
John Jewkes, Jack Wiseman, Ralph Harris, John Brunner, Richard Lynn, and seven company chairmen
1967   (xiii+157pp., £1·00)

4. Taxation—A Radical Approach
A re-assessment of the high level of British taxation and the scope for its reduction
Vito Tanzi, J. B. Bracewell-Milnes, D. R. Myddelton
1970   (xii+130pp., 90p)

5. Economic Issues in Immigration
An exploration of the liberal approach to public policy on immigration
Charles Wilson, W. H. Hutt, Sudha Shenoy, David Collard, E. J. Mishan, Graham Hallett, *with an Introduction by* Sir Arnold Plant
1970   (xviii+155pp., £1·25)

9. The Long Debate on Poverty
Eight essays on industrialisation and 'the condition of England'
R. M. Hartwell, G. E. Mingay, Rhodes Boyson, Norman McCord, C. G. Hanson, A. W. Coats, W. H. Chaloner and W. O. Henderson, J. M. Jefferson
Second Edition with an introductory essay on 'The State of the Debate' by Norman Gash
1974   (xxxii+243pp., £2·50)

11. Regional Policy For Ever?
Essays on the history, theory and political economy of forty years of 'regionalism'
Graham Hallett, Peter Randall, E. G. West
1973   (xii+152pp., £1·80)

14. Inflation: Causes, Consequences, Cures
Discourses on the debate between the monetary and trade union interpretations
Lord Robbins, Samuel Brittan, A. W. Coats, Milton Friedman, Peter Jay, David Laidler
With an Addendum by F. A. Hayek
1974   3rd Impression 1976   (vii+120pp., £2·00)